A FISH
OUT OF
WATER

A FISH OUT OF WATER

9 STRATEGIES EFFECTIVE LEADERS USE
TO HELP YOU GET BACK INTO THE FLOW

GEORGE BARNA

INTEGRITY®
PUBLISHERS
Nashville

A FISH OUT OF WATER

Published in association with Yates & Yates, LLP,
Literary Agents, Orange, California.

All Scripture quotations in this book, except those noted otherwise,
are from The Holy Bible, New International Version.
Copyright © 1973, 1978, 1984, International Bible Society.
Used by permission of Zondervan Bible Publishers.

Quotations marked KJV are from The King James Version of the Bible.

Quotations marked TLB are from The Living Bible,
Copyright © 1971. Tyndale House Publishers, Wheaton, Il.
Used by permission.

Cover Design: Bill Chiaravalle
Interior Design: Inside Out Design & Typesetting

Library of Congress Cataloging-in-Publication Data

Barna, George
 A fish out of water / by George Barna.
  p. cm.
 ISBN 1-59145-017-9 (hardcover)
 ISBN 1-59145-422-0 (trade paperback)
 1. Leadership. 2. Christian leadership. I. Title
 HD57.7.B3664   2002
 303.3'4—dc21   2002068910

Printed in the United States of America
06 07 08 09 10 VG 9 8 7 6 5 4 3 2 1

DEDICATION

This book is dedicated to:

my mother, *Connie Barna,* a Situational leader,

my father, *George Barna,* a Strategic leader, and

my wife, *Nancy Barna,* an Operational leader

—three people who have loved me and led me throughout my life.

CONTENTS

ACKNOWLEDGMENTS

*J*UST AS LEADERSHIP IS MOST EFFECTIVE when it is a team effort, so does the crafting of a book benefit from the involvement of a variety of people. This book has been blessed with the efforts of people whose assistance I would like to acknowledge publicly.

Throughout the years, my team at Barna Research has been instrumental in helping me study, understand, and communicate insights regarding various dimensions of reality. As I worked on this book I was supported by the current Barna Research team: Rachel Ables, Irene Castillo, Jim Fernbaugh, Meg Flammang, Lynn Gravel, Cameron Hubiak, Pam Jacob, David Kinnaman, Jill Kinnaman, Carmen Moore, Dan Parcon, Celeste Rivera, and Kim Wilson. Thank you, team, for your encouragement, your help, and your prayers.

Sealy Yates, Curtis Yates, and John Eames, from Yates & Yates, have served as my agents, capably helping me to navigate the strange and wonderful world of publishing. I am grateful for their initiative, wisdom, and professionalism in handling the business end of this work.

A Fish Out of Water

I am excited about the growing relationship with my friends at Integrity Publishing. I have known Byron Williamson and Joey Paul for years and am pleased to be partnering in this and forthcoming projects with them. One of the factors that attracted me to Integrity was Rob Birkhead's creative ideas regarding this book; I pray that his vision will come to pass.

Everyone is exposed to great leaders throughout life. I have undoubtedly benefited from the efforts of the tremendous leaders who have invested in me. Among those leaders whose contributions are most significant are Warren Bennis, Bob Buford, Chuck Colson, Jim Dobson, Larry DeWitt, Wally Erickson, Archie Freeman, Barry Hawes, Jack Hayford, Howie Hendricks, Bill Hybels, Les Ingram, Ron Lehmann, Kevin Mannoia, Doug Murren, Larry Osborne, Janet Parshall, Jim and Molly Scott, Ron Sider, Jim Smith, Jim Van Yperen, Luder Whitlock, and Walt Wilson. My life has been enhanced by their input and example.

The most important team of all, though, is my family. For two decades, my wife, Nancy, has helped to lead Barna Research and has taught me much about the operational side of leadership. She has also been a tireless supporter of my efforts to help people and to love God. This book is as much a result of her life as it is of mine. She has been a continual blessing; may she reap her reward a thousandfold. In addition, my daughters, Samantha and Corban, have forever changed my life for the better. What I have not learned about leadership outside the home they have taught me inside the home. Their daily hugs, kisses, and encouraging comments move me to continue to pursue God's calling with passion and energy. A major motivation behind this book is to try to improve the quality of leadership in the world so that their lives might benefit.

Ultimately, everything in life is a spiritual choice. I have chosen to follow Jesus Christ as my Lord and Savior, striving to live a life that honors him and reflects his principles. I pray that this book is an acceptable and pleasing offering of love and obedience to him. If anything good results from this book, may all the glory go to God, all the joy to my family and colleagues, and all the benefit to his church.

—Preface—

> *The greatness of an organization will be directly proportional to the greatness of its leader.*
>
> —HENRY BLACKABY

PREFACE

*I*CAN'T STAND FISHING. The long wait between catches, the slimy bodies, getting the hook out of the creature's bloody, rubbery mouth—well, you get the picture. Ernest Hemingway I'm not.

However, because my daughters love fishing, our family occasionally heads to a nearby dock and fishes for a few hours.

Early one morning the girls were dangling their rods over the railing. I sat on a nearby bench and pondered some difficulties I was facing within our company. The gentle ocean breeze, the lighthearted banter between my wife and daughters, and the absence of telephones and other interruptions were conducive to clarifying reflection.

That is, until both little girls started whooping, frantically reeling in "a big one." After a few minutes of comical effort—have you ever fished with girls who are five and eight?—they managed to secure their prized catches and proudly placed them in their bucket.

Buoyed by their prowess, they baited their hooks anew and expectantly returned to mining the seas. I returned to my bench and tried to pick up my interrupted trail of thought. But it was not to be, due to the flapping of those two fish in the plastic bucket. I couldn't help but consider their plight. If only they had understood their environment better, they could have avoided their fate. If they had just worked together, they might have discerned the trap and swum around it. *If only, if only, if only.* But, no, they had failed to do what was reasonable.

Now each of them was just a fish out of water.

A bolt of insight flooded my mind. In trying to lead my company through a particularly turbulent time, I was doing what people expected me to do, was taking on the entire challenge alone, was losing sight of the underlying purpose of the company, and on and on. The insights suddenly streamed through. News flash: I was a fish out of water.

THIS BOOK IS FOR anyone who leads people, wants to lead people, or knows that they should be leading people. Perhaps you lead through directing a business or a church, a Bible study group or a sports team. You may lead within a military structure or within your family. You may be called upon to provide leadership in a variety of settings, ranging from your hobbies and free-time pursuits to your vocation and community service activities.

Do you ever feel swamped? No matter what type or level of leadership you give to others, leadership is one of the most challenging tasks that we take on during our life. It can also be one of the most rewarding. If you are a leader, I want to help you become more effective by enabling you to anticipate and navigate through the inevitable challenges you will face during your leadership journey.

My research has revealed nine common challenges that confront most leaders during their odyssey. You'll encounter them in the nine chapters that follow. I will share the wisdom and experience of thousands of leaders whose paths I have traced, dissected, and analyzed to help you avoid the same hooks and snags that bruised—and, in some cases, decimated—those leaders.

But I also want you to realize that this is not designed to be some predictable, run-of-the-mill book about leadership skills. In fact, this book will barely touch on skills. I have found that there are five dimensions of leadership that you must own to become an effective leader: calling, comprehension, character, competencies, and consequences.

THE CALLING TO LEADERSHIP

First, you must understand God's calling on your life. He has called some people to be leaders, and most others he has not.

This is an issue of discernment. You cannot force God's calling, nor can you experience a significant life by dismissing or denying his call, whatever it is. Perhaps you have been called to provide leadership to a Girl Scouts troop, a church program, or a small department in a giant multinational corporation. The magnitude of the situation is not important; hearing and obeying his calling is. Ask Jonah what it's like to run from God's calling.

Do you know what God created you for—the specific calling he had in mind when he determined that you would inhabit his planet for a few decades? How obedient have you been in pursuing that calling?

COMPREHENSION FOR LEADERSHIP

Second, you must comprehend what leadership is. Americans have so mythologized and convoluted the notion of leadership that surprisingly few people even understand its essence. It takes insight and maturity to truly grasp God's view of leadership; everything else is a dangerous mind game we play that affects people's lives but fails to glorify God.

The apostle Paul devoted much attention to helping his protégés recognize that authentic leadership is not about position, power, popularity, or perks; it is about obedience and servanthood, resulting in transformation. How deeply do you comprehend the heartbeat of leadership and its significance in God's creation?

Character in Leadership

Next, you must possess the type of character that moves people to trust you to take them places—spiritual, emotional, relational, and intellectual—that they otherwise would not go. God uses those people who, like David, seek to emulate his heart, or people like Paul, who recognize that the minimum qualification for leadership is to emulate Jesus Christ.

Such character demands intense and lifelong commitment. Such character is magnetic; leaders who lack it become actors whose performance only generates an illusion of trustworthiness. Are you fooling people into following you, or does your character compel people to take you seriously?

The Competencies of Leadership

You must also exhibit mastery of competencies that enable you to move people toward meaningful outcomes. These skills and techniques make the art of leadership tangible and real.

The dominant competencies are well known: vision casting, effective communication, motivating participation, mobilizing people into efficient work units, thinking and planning strategically, accumulating the resources required, creating a healthy internal culture, evaluating results and fine-tuning the process, handling conflict, reproducing and training leaders, and delegating tasks to skilled colleagues.

It is a daunting list, but, unlike a calling, these practices can be learned, honed, and perfected. You do not need to be an expert in each of these areas— no leader is—but you must understand your strengths and weaknesses and how to work through and around them. What are the leadership competencies you possess that enable you to make the right things happen?

THE CONSEQUENCES OF LEADERSHIP

Finally, you must take responsibility for the consequences of your leadership. Leaders produce results. Effective leaders produce desirable results in response based upon intentional and strategic efforts to bring those outcomes to fruition. What do you have to show for your leadership efforts—and how well does that fruit reflect the calling and vision and quality that God deserves from your efforts?

There are many fine books that discuss competencies and consequences. There is no sense repeating what others have already communicated so well. In these pages I will emphasize the "overlooked" elements: calling, comprehension, and character. These are the more treacherous mountains that leaders must scale to reach the pinnacle. These are the challenging crosscurrents that leaders must master to reach their desired destination intact and ready for the next leg of the journey.

So, have you ever felt like you were out of your element? I want to help you lead people more effectively, blending your faith in Christ with skills and perspectives that are consistent with Scripture and proven in the world. I will draw from two decades of research with leaders to supply you with practical concepts, strategies, and practices. I want to spare you the pain and suffering that other leaders have needlessly experienced so that you might spend your limited time and resources doing what God has called you to do. I do not want you to be a fish out of water.

Let's dive in.

—GEORGE BARNA

—Introduction—

> *Leaders must help people believe that they can be effective, that their goals are possible of accomplishment, that there is a better future that they can move toward through their own efforts.*
>
> —John Gardner

INTRODUCTION

I HAD JUST FINISHED SPEAKING at a conference of ministry leaders, primarily senior pastors. A dozen or so hurried to the front of the auditorium to talk to me before I left the building. One man kept insisting everyone go before him until he was the only one left.

"I appreciated what you had to say," he began.

I knew this was going to be one of those confrontational conversations that seem to follow me wherever I speak. "But really, I think you put way too much emphasis upon leadership and the significance of the leader. I agree that people need leadership, but if you believe in the sovereignty of God, it's really *his* leadership that we need."

"You are absolutely right," I countered. "Our task is to be obedient servants of God. We are supposed to follow him alone." Then I went on.

"But you have to admit that most people don't really have a clue why God gave them life, why they find themselves in their current circumstances, or how they can add value to the world through their efforts to serve him."

I took a quick breath before my colleague had time to jump in, and continued.

"In fact, most people—even most born-again Christians in America—do not view themselves as God's servants. My exhortations about leadership are based on the notion that God has divinely appointed some individuals to help shape people's lives by understanding what God wants of us and to help lead them there."

"Yeah, but don't you see, George, that ultimately God is in control?" he argued. "Don't you think we're just fooling ourselves into thinking that leaders really make a difference? We should just be preaching the whole Bible and letting it go at that."

I said I understood, but surely he saw that when he preached from the Bible he drew insights about the roles that God's chosen leaders have played in people's lives. The principles of the faith require someone to guide us into consistency with God's dictates.

"Do you really believe that a group of people can live meaningful lives without some understanding of God's vision for them and without an individual whom God has gifted to lead actually pointing the way and shaping the group's thinking and behavior?" I asked.

I did not want to caricature his position, but the superficiality of such a viewpoint troubled me—especially since it was held by someone whom others would expect to provide leadership.

"But I can't trust the people in my church to know how to lead others," he replied, changing the direction of his argument.

That wasn't a problem related to the importance of leadership, I said. That was an issue regarding the quality of leadership—his, as their primary leader and equipper, and theirs, as individuals who must affect the lives of others.

"In fact," I continued, "I'll bet you agree with me on one thing: Leadership has consequences. The better we can prepare people to hear from God, to obey what they hear, and to effectively guide others to comply with what they have heard, the better off we will all be, whether we're leading a church, a business, a sports team, or a family."

Not quite convinced but not sure what to say, my colleague smiled, shook my hand, and thanked me for the exchange. As I packed up my notes and departed, I prayed that he had heard the heart of my argument: Leadership matters and it has consequences.

Introduction

Why We Need Leadership—and to Think Hard About It

The meteoric rise and catastrophic fall of Enron. Sexual abuse and subsequent cover-ups of that abuse by Catholic priests. The swell in church attendance immediately after the September 11, attack on America and the return to pre-attack levels within six weeks. The deadly shootings of teenagers by teenagers at Columbine and other schools. The secret pardoning of dozens of political friends by a former president during his last week in office.

All of these outcomes were the result of decisions—bad decisions—by trusted leaders: business executives, clergy, parents, and a political official, respectively. The choices that leaders make have consequences. Bad choices have bad consequences.

On the other hand, America is a different—and better—nation today because of the leadership provided by President George W. Bush and his team of leaders in response to the September 11 attacks. Houston is a different city because of the incredible leadership of Kirbyjon Caldwell and his team at Windsor Village United Methodist Church who converted an abandoned Kmart and the adjacent property in a tough part of town into a thriving enterprise zone that is being emulated in other cities around the U.S. Employees and customers alike have benefited from the superb leadership of Herb Kelleher at Southwest Airlines, which became a profitable, innovative, fun, and affordable airline during his tenure.

These are also examples of choices by leaders which have had far-reaching consequences—good consequences.

Actions Have Consequences

Like most parents (I hope), my wife and I have worked hard to teach our daughters "actions have consequences." In fact, it has become a mantra of sorts in our household. (Last month, when we heard a speaker use that phrase at church, as soon as the words were out of his mouth both girls immediately turned to me, their eyes big as saucers, amazed that someone else was privy to our family motto.) But if actions have consequences, how much more do the actions of leaders—whose defined purpose is to initiate and guide the actions of groups of people—have consequences?

You could make a compelling argument that the actions of leaders have dramatic consequences because they trigger all other actions (which have consequences) that occur in our world.

> *The successful leader must know when to fight and when to retreat, when to be rigid and when to compromise, when to speak out and when to be silent. He must take the long view—and he must have a clear strategy as well as a goal and a vision. He must take the complete view—he must see the relation of one decision to the others.*
>
> —RICHARD NIXON

I would take the argument a step further and suggest that the actions of leaders who are Christian have the most significant consequences because it is our leadership that affects the visible presence of God and his ways in our world.

God has identified and prepared specific people to be his primary leaders in the world. Some are pastors or people in full-time ministry, but most of them are working in the business world, serving as teachers or coaches, holding public office, involved in a nonprofit venture, or parenting their children. Leadership happens all the time, in many places, in various forms, delivered by different people. What we do, as Christians called to represent God through our leadership, determines the influence of God's ways and his plans on the world in which we have been called to provide an understanding of and adherence to his design for humanity.

Your acts of leadership are not just efforts to earn rewards, create new opportunities, or even to keep God at bay. Your leadership has consequences for you, for the individuals who are directly and indirectly affected by your leading, and for the kingdom of God.

Introduction

SALT AND LIGHT?

I have written several books in recent years that have warned that America was approaching an era of moral and spiritual anarchy, defined as a time when people would essentially be impervious to external influence (laws, rules, peer pressure, family values, church teaching) but in which people would do what they want, when they want, for whatever reasons they want, regardless of the prevailing mores. Many readers have written me asking how such a condition could possibly occur.

There is one simple answer: the absence of God-directed, Spirit-empowered leadership from Christians.

As followers of Christ, you and I are called to emulate Jesus' life and practice his teachings. Jesus instructed his followers—including you and me—to be "the salt of the earth. But if the salt loses its saltiness, how can it be made salty again? It is no longer good for anything, except to be thrown out and trampled by men."[1]

Salt is often preached of as a preservative. But salt is also an agent of change. For instance, sprinkle it on meat and it will change the meat's flavor, color, texture, and shelf life. Spread it on highways and city streets after a snowstorm and it will radically change the snow—into mush. Salt is an aggressive instrument of transformation.

How many Christians do you know in your spheres of influence—at work, at church, in sports leagues, at the hospitals, in the schools, in the inner city, in government—who are aggressive instruments of transformation? How many of the believers with whom you have contact are leading in ways that transcend the preservation of the status quo, who lead in favor of changing everything they can affect to achieve a higher purpose? What are you doing to irrevocably and positively alter that tiny slice of the world that you can influence out of obedience to *who* God made you, *why* he created you, and *how* he wishes to use you?

A Fish Out of Water

Which Leader Is the Most Effective?

My current research on sources of influence in people's lives has also revealed a startling conclusion: The most dramatic effects of Christian leadership do not come from the efforts of pastors, nor do they emanate from activities that happen on church campuses across the land! I am not demeaning pastors and churches; I am simply reporting that at this stage in America's history the impact of Christianity is not primarily felt through the words and behavior of the institutional church and its directors. It is felt more so by the day-to-day ideas, conversations, choices, and activities of individual believers in the workforce, the marketplace, the halls of leisure, and other public forums.

This is neither good nor bad; it is simply fact. But that fact has some powerful implications. It means that if you are a homemaker who homeschools your two children, interacts with your neighbors, and serves at a shelter for battered women, your impact might be as profound as—or even greater than—that of people whose positions require them to provide leadership. It means that if you are a junior-level executive in the manufacturing or service sector, your capacity to influence the direction of the world may be no less significant than that of the pastor of a megachurch or the mayor of your city. Or as the pastor of a small, rural congregation your ability to motivate and mobilize people in response to a vision from God could have a more substantial impact than anything a congressman might accomplish in a decade spent in Washington. It suggests that if you are the coach of a Little League team, your interaction with the twenty boys or girls on your squad may have consequences of unexpected long-term proportions.

Mahatma Gandhi is one of the revered figures of the twentieth century. During his decades of leadership in India, he regularly encouraged people of every caste and class in society to stand up for what they believe and to take risks to bring about desired changes. He affirmed that no matter how small their contribution seemed it would play a role in creating meaningful outcomes. "Whatever you do will be insignificant," he admitted before adding, "but it is very important that you do it."

If you are a follower of Jesus Christ, you will have numerous opportunities throughout your life to lead people in one direction or another. Where will you lead them? What are you doing to prepare for those special moments—those windows of opportunity when you affect the lives of more people than you may ever realize?

CONSIDERING THE OUTCOME

As a Christian, you should lead because you have been called by God to do so. Resist the temptation to move forward simply because the moment is right, the opportunities exist, or the potential for impact is undeniable. Good intentions and overt skills do not qualify you to lead people; God's appointment is the requisite credential.

> *It is not the critic who counts, nor the man who points out how the strong man stumbles or where the doer of deeds could have done them better. The credit belongs to the man who is actually in the arena, whose face is marred by dust and sweat and blood; who strives valiantly . . . who spends himself in a worthy cause.*
> —THEODORE ROOSEVELT

While the potential outcomes should not be the motivating factor for your desire to direct people's efforts, the consequences of leadership are important. Consider these outcomes that spring from effective leadership.

Appropriate Values and Morals

The elements that we consider to be worthwhile and proper do not emerge in a vacuum; our values and morals stem from our character. Leadership is about developing good character. By directing people to reflect on their morals and values we facilitate better choices and behaviors.

A Sense of Purpose and Meaning

Our studies consistently show that tens of millions of Americans, young and old alike, are struggling to gain an understanding of why they exist and what life is about. This is a leadership challenge; the answer lies in our realizing that leadership is about pointing people toward the lifelong pursuit of God's vision. Only as they lock on to that concept will they achieve the sense of direction and significance that every one of us craves.

Clear Understanding of Reality

We are bombarded with more information than we can reasonably process. Many people become overwhelmed with the information and set their sights on simply surviving the onslaught of data and opportunities, hoping to maintain rather than thrive. Leadership is about providing people with reliable contextual interpretation and direction. As leaders we help people make sense of reality—and know how to respond.

Positive Change

When leaders are fulfilling their calling from God, they are making the world a better place. Leadership is about transformation. Whether the changes we facilitate are overtly spiritual or not, every change is ultimately undertaken for spiritual reasons and has eternal implications.

Spiritual Harmony

Godly leadership, which helps people live in ways that honor and glorify God, is consistent with his expressed principles and reconciles his eternal truths with our present circumstances. In other words, leadership is about radical obedience to

God. We strive to empower people to do what is right at the right time. The definition of *rightness* can only come from harmony with God.

Cooperation

Great things happen when people understand each other, discover points of common interest, and work in unity to achieve those shared goals. Leaders develop a pragmatic community infused with love and understanding. Leadership is about collaboration, not competition. We strive to bring people together and achieve synergy through compatible goals, attitudes, and abilities.

Clearly, leadership matters—that is, it makes a lasting difference in the world—when we realize that leadership is about growing people according to God's plan. Knit together by a common purpose (his vision), a common model (Jesus), and a common resource (the Holy Spirit), leaders spark significant consequences in the world.

WHAT MAKES LEADERS FAIL?

After studying leaders and leadership for the past twenty years, I have discovered that surprisingly few people fail as leaders because they lack natural ability, intelligence, energy, skills, or training. More often, we fail as leaders because we try to be someone whom God did not create us to be, because we lack clarity about what leaders must do to facilitate life transformation, or because we do not have the depth of character to help people rise to a better level of existence.

Heart of the Matter

Leadership is the art of serving God by helping his people become more like his Son through the indefatigable pursuit of his vision and values. It is through that pursuit that we become the salt of the earth and that the Christian faith assumes practical meaning and definition in the world.

Just as every person is unique, so are the ways in which God wants each of his chosen leaders to provide direction and purpose to those whom they are called to lead. Leadership requires the application of skills and techniques, but it is ultimately the heart of the leader that determines effectiveness. You can succeed as a leader, in God's eyes, only when you wholeheartedly embrace his call to pursue a vision he has entrusted to you, working in harmony with other leaders for purposes that transcend who you are and what you can hope to accomplish of your own accord.

Don't get me wrong: Competencies are absolutely necessary for someone to be an effective leader. But unless you are crystal-clear about what God has called you to lead people toward, what leadership means to him, and how incredibly significant your character is in gaining God's stamp of approval and people's trust, all the skills and competencies in the world aren't going to get you where you need to go. In the long run, leadership effectiveness hinges on who you are rather than on what you can do. You can learn how to *act* like a leader, but people will not follow you for long unless you *are* a leader.

Every Leader Will Fail—Sometimes

Every leader, regardless of the leadership context, has a healthy backlog of personal stories of leadership crises they have weathered. Even the best leaders I've met, studied, or personally followed have endured times of disaster and failure during their run.

Knowing that even the great ones sometimes struggle has encouraged me to continue to develop as a leader and helped me to understand that the hardships and setbacks that I (and the people following me) endure on my leadership journey are unavoidable. But leaders' tales of temporary defeat, self-doubt, and lost ground also stoked my curiosity about what enables them to maximize their God-given potential.

Introduction

Here's the bottom line: Your leadership adventure will be completely unique, but it will rise and fall according to your capacity to apply the same leadership principles that every other leader must apply. In that journey, there will be  times when you will excel and times when you will fail. Your effectiveness as a leader will largely depend upon how astutely you can anticipate and prepare for a relative handful of challenges that are coming your way.

> *Consensus is no substitute for leadership; character is formed in the midst of people in crisis, not in solitude or in prosperity.*
> —CHARLOTTE BEERS

So, exactly what are the challenges, opportunities, and obstacles that hinder people from becoming effective, godly, transformational leaders?

The nine chapters that follow will each focus on a particular challenge that our research reveals to be among the most common and demanding enigmas facing leaders today.

Chapter 1: The organization is still afloat, but it seems like we're drifting about aimlessly. Administration, teaching, management, and organizing are not synonymous with leadership. You can orchestrate an efficient activity or organization without leading it to anyplace of significance. What you may be missing is a clear understanding of what genuine leadership is and what difference that insight makes to how you think, act, and affect lives.

Chapter 2: God did not call me to be a Big Fish, but people sometimes rely upon me for leadership anyway. You need to recognize the difference between situational and habitual leadership. Most people are not called to full-time leadership, but everyone needs at least a few basic tools to facilitate a reasonable response during those situations in which they must provide leadership. There are certain elements that situational leaders need to understand and certain strategies for *getting by* in these situations—kind of the Cliffs Notes version for acing the exam.

Chapter 3: I just can't handle all the pressures and expectations people have of me as a leader. I don't know enough, and I can't possibly do all that people need. Believe it or not, this is an incredibly healthy crisis to experience. At some point, once you understand what people demand of their leaders, you will want to run and hide. But this is God's way of humbling you into realizing your dependence upon him and your need to partner with other leaders who possess some helpful leadership traits that are not your strength. You need to convert your limitations into assets by discovering your leadership aptitude and developing a team of leaders whose capacity exceeds the sum of the parts.

Chapter 4: There are more great opportunities out there than I can shake a stick at. I don't know where to start or which direction to swim in. One of the most common downfalls of leaders is their inability to clearly define God's vision for their activity. We rarely lack opportunities; what we lack is clarity regarding God's intentions for us, and how that should define what we pursue. Effective leaders are in sync with God's vision and use that insight as the centerpiece of their leadership process.

Chapter 5: I'm worried about my skill levels. Maybe people won't follow me if they sense I'm not up to the task. If you believe that people's support of leaders is based mostly on leaders' skill levels, think again. Our research shows that their allegiance is due to who leaders are rather than what they can do: They forgive a leader whose abilities are still developing, but they abandon leaders of inferior morals and ethics. There is no substitute for good character in leaders; invest in it.

Chapter 6: I'm working hard, I'm doing this for the right reasons and in the right ways, but nobody seems to be following. What's wrong? We regularly focus on training leaders, but who trains people to be effective followers? That's a leader's job—and, for impact, it must be a priority.

Chapter 7: I want everyone to join my school of fish and stick close. That means I can't risk upsetting people by my decisions or my style. If you want to be popular, become an entertainer; if you're called to lead, get used to ruffling people's feathers (to mix metaphors). The two primary functions of leaders are to create conflict and resolve conflict. To be effective, you must know when and how to use conflict as a tool for facilitating growth and progress.

Chapter 8: Leadership is so demanding that something has to give. For the time being, I'm going to have to sacrifice my own spiritual development until my schedule frees up. Such thinking may fly in the world, but it falls flat in the kingdom. There is no such thing as an effective Christian leader who puts his or her spiritual development on the back burner. In a spiritual battle you regularly restock your spiritual ammunition. Unless you are intensely devoted to continually cultivating your relationship with Christ, people have no valid reason to follow you—and you have no business striving to lead God's people.

Chapter 9: I started this company and I ran it successfully for years. But lately, I seem to have lost my touch. Bank on it: You will encounter times when the skills and practices that got you where you are will not get you where you need to go. Understanding the life cycles of organizations and which type of leadership best fits at each stage of development will help you progress.

CAN YOU RELATE to some of these situations and challenges? Every time I've been bogged down in one of these states, I've felt like a fish out of water—and longed for a way to get back in a life-sustaining environment in which I could be effective at doing what God created me to do.

Leaders are strategic. That means they anticipate the future and prepare for it. Leaders hate surprises and despise lack of preparation for predictable circumstances. My objective is to help you anticipate and prepare for the predictable, virtually inevitable leadership challenges that research indicates you will have to deal with at some point on your leadership journey. You need to understand how to lead within the limits that define you: Accept those limits, adapt to them, and succeed because of them rather than in spite of them. That's the leadership philosophy that you'll find in the Bible. Discover that subtle but special place where you balance your faith and your God-given leadership capacity. Use your talents and gifts to become a mature, God-honoring Christian and an effective leader at the same time.

A Fish Out of Water

If you master the knowledge and strategies outlined in this book, you can take your group—your family, your business, your department, your church, your class, or your ball team—to the next level. Ignore these strategies and you are likely to crash and burn—and you will probably take others down with you.

These are not magical, can't-miss steps, but they have proven themselves time after time, in situation after situation, because they are based on God's timeless wisdom and his perfect principles. Naturally, their impact depends on how well you execute them, but you must understand their place and substance in order to implement them adequately. If God has called you to lead, you are pursuing a wonderful but difficult life. By intelligently and purposefully addressing the challenges that you face in leadership, you can raise the water level for God's people.

— I —

> *Many an institution is very well managed and very poorly led. It may excel in the ability to handle each day all the routine inputs yet may never ask whether the routine should be done at all. . . . Leaders are people who do the right thing; managers are people who do things right.*
>
> —WARREN BENNIS

CHAPTER ONE

Somebody Has to Be the Big Fish

MARTIN HAD BEEN THE CEO of a small business in the Southwest for nearly five years when I first met him. After completing his MBA, he had worked his way up the authority chain in several midsized corporations before snagging his current post. His predecessor had been an organizational disaster, so it wasn't hard for Martin to gain superstar status in the eyes of his coworkers. In relatively short order he put some important operational systems in place, solved a few vexing personnel problems, clarified the job responsibilities of key employees, built positive relationships with board members, and established benchmarks against which performance could be measured. He was well liked, had created a pleasant working environment, and frequently encouraged his people to stick to their plans. Employees and customers alike were impressed his demeanor and his integration of faith and behavior.

Martin was troubled, though, by a nagging belief that something important was missing. The company's gross revenues and profits were stagnant, although that was widely attributed to a declining economy and a soft industry. Few employees seemed to care much about the company's standing, which insiders dismissed as a reflection of the general state of malaise among workers everywhere. But it didn't add up: a company with a quality product, a well-trained staff, strong corporate name recognition, and sufficient production capacity for growth—with little evidence of growth, or even the immediate potential to grow.

After a couple of intense discussions together, Martin's problem became clear. Although the company had a handful of genuine leaders, none of them really understood what leaders do. They were serving as managers and administrators rather than leaders. Their erroneous assumptions about leadership were undermining their ability to provide the environment and resources that the firm needed to kick things into gear. They had the tools; they simply did not know how to use them.

NAVIGATING A DILEMMA LIKE MARTIN'S

Martin is not the first leader to have an uneasy feeling that something's amiss without the ability to put his finger on the precise dilemma. Those of us who analyze organizational circumstances know that there are usually no simple solutions to such situations, either.

For instance, in Martin's case there could have been myriad problems holding back his firm in addition to the theories already mentioned. In other communications he listed a possible lag time between when he made his internal improvements and when the effect of those improvements kicked in. All of these could have contributed to his company's lackadaisical performance.

Other possibilities existed, too, which he was encouraged to explore. The quality of his company's products might have deteriorated or failed to keep pace with innovations in their industry. Competitors may have gained an edge in pricing. Customer service might have lost ground. The company's marketing efforts—sales, advertising, and promotions—might not be up to speed. Distribution channels might be delaying product delivery or causing the product to be insufficiently convenient to satisfy consumers. Salary and benefits packages might not be rewarding employees commensurate to current marketplace trends. Add to these a host of internal idiosyncrasies and you can understand how tough it is to determine how to re-energize and refocus a group of people.

In the end, however, when the basics are solid—that is, the product is viable; it is easily accessible to the target market; the cost of the product, service, or experience is reasonable; and the target market is sufficiently aware of its existence—then the issue is likely to be even more fundamental.

In Martin's firm, like so many others, there was a serious leadership deficit. Martin and his fellow executives lacked an accurate understanding of the substance of leadership, even though most of them had advanced degrees and had studied leadership. None of them grasped what it means to be a leader. Not surprisingly, when they were initially informed that their barrier was due to the lack of leadership, they resisted the idea.

How Do You Define Leadership?

Further digging revealed that Martin and his team had considered the possibility of bad leadership being the problem—and soundly rejected that possibility. Why? Because they misdefined leadership.

How do you define leadership? What is it? In real, practical terms, what does a leader do? Take a moment and write down how you would define leadership. You might find that simple assignment tougher than imagined.

What Leadership Is Not

My research shows that more often than not, people confuse leadership with other important but different practices or results.

Among the most common misperceptions are the following:

Leadership is influence. To be effective, a leader must have influence. But influence

5

is a product of great leadership; it is not synonymous with it. You can have influence in a person's life without leading him anywhere. Just think about salespeople (they influence purchases but are not exhibiting leadership by closing the sale); teachers (they may convey information that influences our understanding or stimulates us to action, but they do not necessarily provide vision and direction that leads us to an intended outcome); or doctors (after they diagnose your illness and prescribe a medicine, they have influenced your behavior and health, but they are not directing your life to any extent).

To equate leadership with influence is to set the bar too low and to set people up for failure. It produces "leaders" who are simply motivators and informants. A true leader has a much deeper impact.

Leadership is getting important things done efficiently. A common misinterpretation is that leadership is the same as management. Management exists to make things happen efficiently. Leadership provides direction to produce effectiveness. Warren Bennis and Burt Nanus have suggested that managers do things right, while leaders do the right things.[1] That description may not go far enough. Leaders do the right thing, for the right reason, at the right time. In fact, my research indicates that because leaders are focused on doing the right thing, they are often inefficient in their work—and yet, because of their transformational focus, their effectiveness is not hindered by their inefficiency. The best leaders compensate by surrounding themselves with others who enhance the efficiency quotient without altering the direction or minimizing the impact of the organization.

Leadership is based on controlling the decision-making apparatus through a consolidation of power and position. This definition introduces two of the most dangerous words in organizational realities: control and power. Leadership is not about gaining control; it is about releasing control to people who share a common vision of the future and are united in their pursuit of that vision. Likewise, leadership is not about coalescing power; it is about distributing power to those who are committed to that common vision. Great leaders empower and release rather than dictate and confine.

Somebody Has to Be the Big Fish

Leaders gain the opportunity to lead by becoming the most popular person among peers.
Leadership is not a popularity contest. In fact, I've learned that great leaders ride
a popularity roller coaster, sometimes popular and sometimes unpopular. Many
of our most effective leaders have been quite unpopular because their primary
focus is to cause people and circumstances to change—and people hate to
change, even when it's in their best interests.

Many individuals who have had a lasting, positive legacy from their era
endured times of crushing public rejection in spite of the laudable transformation that their leadership produced. (Rudy Giuliani of New York City is a
wonderful example—someone who is widely credited with having turned
around the feel, the environment, and even the self-image of the city, yet had
numerous vocal critics—until he silenced them all in the weeks following the
September 11 tragedy through his powerful and sensitive leadership.) If you
want to be a leader, make sure you can handle confrontation and rejection; it is
almost an inevitable side effect of leadership.

A DEFINITION OF LEADERSHIP

But if leadership is more than influence, different than efficiency, resists accumulating control and power, and typically defies popularity, then what is
leadership? Try this perspective:

> Leadership is the process of motivating, mobilizing, resourcing, and
> directing people to passionately and strategically pursue a vision
> from God that a group jointly embraces.

A leader gets people excited about God's vision. This is substantive motivation,
not the up-now, down-tomorrow superficial motivation that comes from pumping
up people's self-esteem or extols one-dimensional dreams of grandeur to which
people might unrealistically aspire. Leaders enable people to be genuinely inspired

7

by the only thing that is worth getting out of bed for each morning: lives dedicated to fulfilling God's unique and worthwhile purpose for us. The only way leaders can get their groups to sustain their energy over the long haul is to give them a vision that justifies a long-term commitment. That vision will not emphasize profits, popularity, or power. It will always come back to life transformation.

> *People don't follow titles. They follow leaders. Provide them with compelling leadership and they will change the world.*
>
> —SOURCE UNKNOWN

Great leaders also mobilize people around a compelling cause (in other words, the vision) because there is always greater strength and lasting impact from a joint effort than from a solo effort. No matter what the particular vision from God may be, it transcends the capacity of a single person. Effectiveness, then, demands that leaders bring together people of like minds and hearts to blend their abilities toward bringing the vision to reality.

Life-changing outcomes do not happen, however, without resources. How many great ideas have died quiet deaths because of an absence of resources? Vision becomes reality when a sufficient body of human, financial, spiritual, intellectual, and physical resources has been accumulated for application in the pursuit of the vision. The leader is responsible for identifying the resources required, determining how to get them, and implementing the acquisition plan.

Pursuing the Vision

The most obvious leadership task is to direct all of these entities—resources as well as people's passion, energy, and skills—in a strategic manner to bring the vision to life. The leader gives shape to the parcel of resources to produce the desired outcome. Such direction happens through public and private communication, conceptualization and planning, evaluation, team building, behavioral modeling, and prayer.

You don't have to possess a charismatic personality or be a spellbinding speaker or hold degrees from Harvard and Princeton. But you must be able to focus on doing the right things, for the right reasons, at the right time.

> *The leader must know, must know that he knows, and must make it abundantly clear to those about him that he knows.*
>
> —CLARENCE RANDALL

Don't overlook the most important element in all of this activity: Everything that a Christian leader does relates to God's vision. Without that vision as the centerpiece of your leadership, you can lead people only to chaos or irrelevance. It is God's vision and his vision alone that provides meaning to your life, purpose to your leadership, and enduring enthusiasm to people's involvement.

God's vision is a leader's oxygen. Without it, you can get by for a while, but eventually you will die a painful death.

Lost without a Vision

In essence, leadership is about helping people make sense and achieve purpose out of life. On a national scale, American society is in moral, spiritual, and emotional turmoil today because we have lost our sense of what constitutes truth and value. We have exchanged an eternal perspective for a temporal, immediate point of view that seduces us but leaves us empty. How did that happen? We followed leaders who diverted our attention and turned our minds and hearts toward things that do not and cannot satisfy our deepest longings and ultimate calling and cannot provide us with meaningful experience.

In other words, we have lost our way because we followed leaders who directed us toward human visions rather than godly vision. Consequently, as a nation we have lost our sense of purpose and have convinced ourselves that the daily pleasures and short-term outcomes we seek will restore our sense of purpose.

On a more individual level, this challenges you, as a leader, to stay riveted to the right things, for the right reasons, in the right time frame. You help people make sense out of life by leading them to focus on God's vision, inhabiting that purpose, and enabling them to experience the pleasure of knowing and dedicating themselves to seeing his ends achieved through their individual and joint efforts. As one of God's chosen leaders, you play an incredibly important role in helping people's lives to reach their potential by helping them to elevate God's perspectives and purpose.

As you consider what it means for you to be a leader—what you do and why you do it—answer these questions:

How effectively are you stimulating people's minds and hearts with a compelling presentation of God's vision? How adroitly are you discerning people's abilities and bringing them together to cooperate in the pursuit of the vision? How well prepared are your followers to make things happen that will honor God and bring his vision to fruition? And how intentional and strategic have you been in developing concepts, approaches, and tactics that your people can follow toward achieving the goals that relate to the vision?

> *Leadership is not something that is done to people, like fixing your teeth. Leadership is unlocking people's potential to become better.*
> —BILL BRADLEY

MANY IN POSITIONS OF LEADERSHIP ARE NOT LEADING

To be even more direct, the truth is that most pastors are not leading their congregations anywhere. They are teaching truth, supervising staff and volunteers, and marketing their services to the public—all of which is good, necessary, and laudable. But they are not casting God's compelling vision for their ministry to people and directing the flow of energy and resources in a single-minded manner toward that new reality. They need to lead or step aside so someone called by God can provide the leadership that his people desperately need.[2]

Millions of business executives are not leading their businesses. Though they are paid to lead and have a leadership title, they focus on organizing, problem solving, and outlasting the competition.

Just as teaching truth in the church is good but inadequate, so are organizing and problem solving beneficial but insufficient in a business. Organization facilitates efficiency, but it does not automatically produce effectiveness. Problem solving is most often a means of survival rather than a path to transformation. A business without leadership will exist for a season, then dissipate; it will not be able to withstand the ravages of a rapidly changing, increasingly demanding culture.

Although I do not have sufficient statistical evidence, I also believe that most elected officials are engaged in maintaining pre-existing systems, mollifying their varied constituencies, and investing in personal posturing but providing little evidence of true leadership.

But the most important question relates to you: Are you really leading people or are you simply occupying the leader's office while failing to fulfill its responsibilities and exploit its opportunities?

Churches teach too much material and offer too many programs that are disconnected from God's vision for his people in that place. Businesses spend too much time running the numbers, writing the personnel manuals, and seeking to steal away market share without a compelling reason to do so as found in God's calling to the organization. Government officials and agencies create too many laws that lack a coherent and godly vision. Are you contributing to the problem or introducing a new way by leading people toward a compelling, godly vision of a better tomorrow because you understand genuine leadership and are committed to providing such direction?

QUESTIONS THAT MAY IDENTIFY A PROBLEM OF DEFINITIONS

To determine whether you truly understand what leadership is about, initiate the following diagnosis. Ask yourself these questions—and provide honest answers.

The pattern that emerges will give you insight into whether comprehension of the essence of leadership is the root problem with which you're struggling.

What gets you most excited about the privilege of leading people? For some it will be the public acclaim; for others it's the adrenaline rush of making decisions and taking risks. For a few it will be the prestige of the position; still others will refer to the power or influence that accompany leadership opportunities. Many corporate leaders are driven by a *need* to produce profits.

None of these answers is inherently bad—all can be used for appropriate ends—but none of them is ultimately the right reason for leading. You lead as an act of obedience to God in the hope of honoring him through the pursuit of his vision. Your purpose is to help people's lives gain true meaning and greater depth as they seek his ends. Knowing that you played a role in making people's lives more significant and giving them the joy of experiencing God's presence, purposes, and power should send a tingle down your spine.

When you make tough decisions on behalf of the organization, what is the primary filter through which your choices are made? Is it the statistical measures of performance (such as money or customer base)? Is it feelings about what might work or be most satisfying? Or is it a sense of responsibility to implement the vision and build up God's people in the process?

When you motivate people to get involved in tasks, on what basis do you motivate them? Is it your charismatic personality? Is it compelling communications about how you could be more successful together if you pursued a particular course of action? Do you use peer pressure, competitive positioning, maybe even guilt? Is your emphasis on the traditional motivational approach of building them up emotionally and psychologically? Or do you get people jazzed about the vision and how they play a significant role in bringing it to reality?

Effective leaders enable people to own the vision as if they had thought it up by themselves and clarify how the individual's gifts and abilities will contribute to making the vision a special legacy.

When you have to generate the resources to get the job done, what is your clinching argument founded upon? Do you appeal to someone's logic? Do you push them to help out of a sense of justice or perhaps on the basis of your personal relationship? I hope you focus on how those resources will change people's lives, how the investment of those resources will honor God and carry out his vision.

Your Honest Answers

Think about the last time somebody asked you what you do for a living. How did you describe what you do? Did the language and tone you used reflect a leadership mentality or a producer mentality? As you quickly composed the response in your mind, were you thinking tasks or overarching purpose? No matter how you positioned yourself, what did you perceive yourself to be?

Perhaps you will discover that your understanding of leadership is on the mark, and you are consistently thinking and behaving like a true leader. If that is the case, and your organization is plateaued or stalled, it suggests that your challenges are likely related to other factors: the levels of excellence and consistency in the execution of your tasks, environmental challenges that may be beyond your control or require some radical actions to alter the environment, or a level which needs a leader with a higher level of competencies. (If the latter is the case, read chapter 9.)

The most common outcome, however, is the revelation that you are in a position of leadership but you are not perceiving, interpreting, and responding like a leader. In other words, you are filling a position but not meeting the needs that the position is designed to fulfill and that must be fulfilled if the organization is to have any present meaning and lasting impact. If that is true for you, your highest priority—right now!—must be to alter that reality and enhance your leadership immediately.

To do so, take whatever time and resources are necessary to reformulate your understanding of the following:

- who you are (*a leader called by God*);

- the practice of leadership *(providing specific individuals with motivation, direction, partners, and resources);*
- what your leadership is about *(transforming lives through the pursuit of a specific vision from God);*
- what it will take to raise your personal leadership quotient to the higher level *(personal changes that will result in changing the world);* and
- how you will begin to implement your newfound insights *(this is my plan for being the leader God called me to be in this time and place).*

After you have worked through these considerations, get together with one or two other leaders you know and trust—and who know you and would jump at the chance to help you. Run your thoughts by them for some objective feedback—don't do this in a vacuum. (Remember: operating in that vacuum may have gotten you to where you are in the first place.)

Change yourself, then help others to change the world—the right way, for the right reasons, at the right time.

Uncomfortable Questions

- Do the people you are trying to lead think of you as a boss, a pastor, a friend, a manager, just another employee, an egomaniac, or an effective leader? Why?
- Make a list of the activities you carried out today in your leadership position. Which ones relate to motivating people to pursue God's vision? Which ones relate to how you mobilized people around the vision? Which were designed to amass the resources required to make the vision real? Which reflected your determination to give people guidance on the direction to take toward making the vision real? How many times today did you allude to the vision in conversation with those whom you were leading? How many times did you think about the vision when you were making important decisions?

- Who is the most effective leader whom you have ever followed? What qualities made that person so effective? Who is the least effective leader you have ever followed? What made that person so ineffective? What qualities do you share with the most effective leader? What leadership qualities do you have in common with the least effective leader with whom you have been associated?

—2—

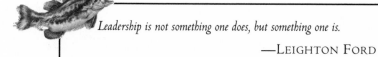

Leadership is not something one does, but something one is.

—LEIGHTON FORD

CHAPTER TWO

Everybody Is a Leader—Sort Of

OB AND HEATHER have two young children: Allen, 11, and Mary, 8. They live comfortably in a suburb of Detroit where Bob works as a vice president of marketing and Heather works as a checkout clerk at a retail store. They are deeply involved in their church and in the Christian school that both of their children attend.

Because of his job, Bob travels often. The family has become used to his absences despite the added pressure they place on Heather while he is away. During one of Bob's trips to Europe, Allen had an incident at school with another boy who was two years older. After some verbal sparring, the two boys squared off and fought on the school playground until a couple of teachers broke up the melee. Allen got the worst of it, as evidenced by his black eye and numerous scrapes. Both boys were suspended from school.

Heather was called at work. When she arrived at school she found Allen sitting dejectedly in the principal's office with an ice pack against his swelling eye. Tears formed in her own eyes as she listened to the principal's summary of the events. The drive home was marked by a frigid silence as she struggled to disentangle her own emotions—disappointment in her son's behavior, the desire to nurse him to physical and emotional health, and the duty to be a strong parent in the face of such a challenge.

Once they got home, Heather sat Allen on the living room sofa and peppered him with questions as she re-dressed his wounds. After fifteen minutes of interaction they prayed together. She told her youngster he should forgive the other boy, avoid him whenever possible, take care of his injuries, and forget about the disagreement that had caused the fight so that he could move on in life. "It's just one of those things that happen when boys grow up," she explained to her son. "It's best to just get on with your life as if nothing happened."

Two days later Bob returned from Europe, fatigued by jet lag and job stress. His customary casual debriefing with his wife brought to light Allen's conflict. This news immediately got his adrenaline pumping and ignited a barrage of questions about the incident and its aftermath.

Whereas Heather had seen the conflict as a tragedy to be healed, Bob viewed it as an event that would help shape his son's life. He was intent upon loving his son to maturity by empowering him to address the situation strategically.

The following day, Bob scheduled meetings with the school principal, the teachers who were involved in the incident, and the parents of Allen's nemesis. With Allen by his side the entire day, he helped flesh out the issues, discussed the actions that had been taken, evaluated their merit, and addressed the need for permanent changes that would prevent future flareups of the same nature. It was an exhausting day, but Bob was committed to providing the leadership that the other adults involved had failed to put forth.

"Allen needs to understand that this is not just a schoolyard tussle that can be brushed off. There are matters of principle, morals, and faith underlying the circumstance, and we have to put these things in perspective," explained Bob after resolutions had been identified.

Bob acknowledged that it was tough to sit face to face with the people involved and walk through the ugly scene again. But he wouldn't be able to live with himself knowing he did not guide his son in how a Christian handles conflict and chaos.

"This is my responsibility to him, to his community, and to Christ. This is a learning moment for him, but also a defining moment for the school and those of us who proclaim Christ as our Savior. This was not just a fight. It was about who he is as a follower of Christ and how his Christian principles get applied in his life."

Spoken like a true leader.

THE DIFFERENCE BETWEEN BOB AND HEATHER

You probably relate better to one or the other of these parents. As you might have surmised, they are very different kinds of leaders. Bob is what I describe as a *habitual* leader; Heather, like most men and women, is a *situational* leader. The contrast in orientation explains why each reacted so differently to the same situation.

It is true that every person is a leader—sort of. How much stock you place in the notion that all people are leaders depends on what you mean by *leader.*

Two decades of leadership research have enabled me to draw the following conclusions.

- *First, there are two types of leaders: those who are called and gifted by God to lead other people and cannot help but be a leader under pressure, and those who lead only because they are forced to do so in a given situation.*

For habitual leaders it is their habit to lead others, whether asked to or not; they cannot repress the urge to lead. Situational leaders, the most common type, are individuals who have not been called or gifted by God to devote their life to leadership but must occasionally provide leadership in circumstances that arise and demand guidance. This is the grudging, infrequent leadership that most of us provide to others.

- *Second, habitual leaders are born that way.* You cannot be taught or trained to become a habitual leader. These are individuals who were conceived in order to provide leadership. It is who they are. Their gift is not the understanding and practicing of techniques that look like leadership. Leadership is in their spiritual DNA. The Lord has crafted them for the purpose of directing others toward his vision and ends, thereby enabling them to see the world through an entirely different lens and to respond quite naturally but differently to every circumstance.

- *Third, situational leaders who are placed in positions that require constant leadership will hurt themselves and many others by masquerading as leaders.* They are the ultimate fish out of water. They may learn how to get by in those moments when they must lead, but it will always be an uncomfortable, unnatural struggle for them.

- *Finally, effectiveness in life (and leadership) comes from acceptance of how God "wired" you.* You must strive for self-understanding and anticipate potential situations so that you may be properly prepared to maximize your unique potential for God's purposes.

Responding As God Wired You To

Heather is a loving mom. She immediately came to the aid of her child and helped him to gain perspective and begin his healing process. Her concern was for the immediate safety and comfort of her child. She saw further confrontation as a continuation of the situation that had threatened her son. Her assumption was that Allen needed to distance himself from the individuals involved and put the entire matter out of his mind so he could enjoy life and experience all the goodness that God has in store for him.

Bob is a loving dad. He immediately recognized that the incident meant more than bruised skin and school suspension. His natural inclination was to create appropriate meaning from the incident and to take whatever measures were necessary to gain clarity, comprehension, and closure. A fight is never just a fight; the conflict always relates to larger moral, ethical, spiritual, and interpersonal issues that must be resolved—and that cannot be resolved by hoping they will "take care of themselves."

Both of these individuals responded in concert with their giftedness and calling from God. Our natural response in such situations is a reflection of who we are, as determined by God. For example, a teacher offers information and context. A mercy giver offers empathy and love. An administrator suggests changes in the process that led to the situation. Your reaction reflects your spiritual gifts and your natural talents and abilities.

Innately Guiding toward God's Outcomes

Habitual leaders who are Christian innately seek to provide direction that guides people to God's desired outcomes by facilitating life transformation and obedience to God. Success to a Christian leader is not prestige, fame, wealth, or power. It is pleasing God by enabling his vision to be fulfilled and by consistently helping people to become more Christlike in the process.

Habitual leaders know that their job will not be easy, yet they address it with anticipation, hope, and energy. Although all leaders have their moments of doubt and weakness, habitual leaders typically cannot imagine anything better than being able to lead people to a better future.

Responding to Circumstance

Situational leaders give direction because circumstances demand it. Consequently, rather than seeking to change the world through their actions, they more often strive "not to blow it." Surviving the circumstance is more often the entry-level mind-set of the situational leader. To most situational leaders, success is the avoidance of failure.

These individuals accept leadership because they feel they have no choice and see the responsibility as a difficult burden, if not a nuisance. They accept the assignment with resignation and get by the best they can. Often that attitude of reluctance and the hope of avoiding future episodes of leadership challenges prevents them from experiencing the joy of effective situational leadership.

Most situational leaders don't seem to realize that they don't have to be habitual leaders to enjoy the leadership process and its outcomes. Just as you don't have to play like Rubenstein to gain enjoyment from playing the piano or be da Vinci to enjoy creating art, neither do you have to be a respected habitual leader to enjoy leading people for God's purposes. You may wind up being more of a technician than a true visionary, but when God can use you to deliver positive consequences in a person's life, why quibble?

One in Eight

Understanding which you are—habitual leader or situational leader—is of critical importance. Most people are situational leaders; I estimate that just one out of every eight individuals has been created for and called by God to habitual leadership.

Acknowledging that God has not made you a habitual leader is not a sign of diminished value, inferiority, or personal deficiency; everyone has talent, but not everyone has a talent for everything. While leadership is not their primary calling, situational leaders provide significant moments of leadership to others. If you are one of the tens of millions of situational leaders in the world, how do you master and maximize those unexpected leadership moments when it is not naturally in your mind and heart to do so?

The Call to Leadership

To develop your ability as a situational leader, you must first be certain that God has not designed you to be a habitual leader. This knowledge is important because the preparation a habitual leader goes through—not to mention the way he or she lives—is quite different from that of a situational leader.

To discern which type of leader you are, consider these five factors.

Determine your spiritual gifts. Scripture is quite clear that God gives every believer special, supernatural abilities that are to be used throughout life for the purposes of his kingdom. There are various gifts tests that you can take that may help you better understand this component of your composure. Knowing your gifts—and our research shows that only one quarter of all born-again adults actually know what their gifts are—will help you better understand yourself, God's design for your life, and how to maximize your service to him.[1] Has God given you the spiritual gift of leadership?

Identify God's vision for your life. Because you were created to know God intimately and to demonstrate the sincerity of your relationship with him by loving him with your heart, mind, soul, and strength, you must take the time to understand what he is uniquely calling you to do through the gifts, abilities, education, relationships, and experiences he has given you. (In chapter 4 we will look more specifically at how you discern the vision and apply it in your life.) One of the hallmarks of habitual leaders is their laserlike focus on that vision; it is the oxygen they breathe that gives them energy and enthusiasm. But God has a unique vision for each of his creatures as we work together in the incredibly intricate puzzle of his creation. Does his vision call for you to serve as a leader?

Discern what you're most passionate about. Undoubtedly you have discovered that people are most passionate about the things that matter most to them. This is a key insight because if God has called you to leadership, you will exude tremendous passion for the act of leading. You will seek new insights on the practice of leadership, enjoy spending time with other leaders, automatically evaluate the leadership of others to discover new techniques and knowledge, and seek to associate with those organizations that esteem or provide genuine leadership. Are you passionate about the idea, the practice, and the development of leadership?

Look at your life experience for clues. It has been suggested by theologians that there are no accidents in life; every life event has divine implications and purpose. This means that if you are to serve as a habitual leader, your labyrinth of life experiences will have been designed to equip you to lead people.

For some individuals, this has been obvious: invitations to enroll in leadership development programs, earning academic degrees in leadership, promotions to leadership positions in the organizations they associate with, and so forth. For others, the path may not have been so clear-cut. Perhaps there were Outward Bound–type experiences or other group endeavors that were not centered on you but began to deposit skills and concepts in your mind and heart that would be valuable leadership resources. Maybe someone who mentored you was tacitly passing on ways of thinking that would enable you to lead more proficiently in the future.

Sometimes God simply places you in situations where you may observe great leaders applying their gifts or where you have to rise to the occasion to provide what you had assumed was merely situational leadership. As you reflect on your life experiences, what has God done to prepare you for leadership?

Ask those who know you best. A helpful indicator of the type of leader you are comes from the observations and comments of those who know you best. None of us has the ability to objectively assess who we are or how we perform. (If you doubt this, sit in on a dozen or so job interviews or employee performance reviews. The disconnect between self-perception and reality is frequently alarming!) Gaining an outsider's perspective can help validate your self-perceptions—if your confidants are willing to be honest and forthright with you. Do your closest friends view you as a leader?

It is also helpful to gain the objective perspective of true leaders. Leaders know leaders. They can sense others who have the same mind and heart that they possess—and appreciate those qualities and typically strive to encourage other leaders to employ their gift. Good leaders will take your earnest questions about your leadership calling and capacity seriously, for they know that misleading a person in this area produces dire consequences. When you ask proven leaders to assess your leadership capacity, how do they respond?

Put together, these inputs should provide you with a pretty accurate self-portrait concerning whether God has called you to habitual leadership.[2] If it appears that he has not done so, don't fret; you'll still have hundreds if not thousands of opportunities to lead people during your lifetime. If it seems that he has ordained you to serve people through leadership, accept the challenge and invest yourself in being the best leader you can be.

MAXIMIZING YOUR SITUATIONAL LEADERSHIP

If you discover that you are a situational leader, you still have a responsibility to serve people the best you can in those situations. How can you do that?

It may be helpful to recognize that there are different levels of leadership that people provide. There seem to be three levels on which you might lead: the micro, mezzo, or macro levels.

Micro, Mezzo, or Macro

Most situational leaders provide micro-level leadership—that is, direction and guidance related to individual or localized needs.

Mezzo-level leadership is often considered the training ground for great leaders. Mezzo-

> *To be a good leader you have to be a romantic. Because then you not only want to make a difference, you imagine that you can.*
> —RICHARD NORTH PATTERSON

level leadership is that which affects a wider group of people and has broad social implications. These are individuals whose leadership may affect an entire town, county, or region. Once they prove themselves at such a level, many leaders then take on macro-level leadership, in which their actions and decisions impact the behavior and lives of many people in a very dispersed geographic area.

Many situational leaders become paralyzed over the potential of leading large groups of people or making world-changing decisions. More likely, though, God will prompt you to provide leadership that affects one or a just few lives at a time. Yet, the basic elements involved in leadership are the same, whether you will lead at a micro, mezzo, or macro level. It is the intensity and implications of your challenge that will differ. In other words, everyone needs to know the leadership fundamentals, although we will be asked to employ them in different ways and divergent situations.

You may also have been anxious about having to motivate, mobilize, resource, and direct people toward a common vision from God, as was suggested that true leaders do. For a situational leader, the notion of vision may look quite different, since your leadership is related to a specific circumstance rather than an ongoing relationship and long-term outcome.

In situational leadership, the desired outcome may be generally described as seeking to bring glory to God by fostering obedience to biblical principles, empowering his people to pursue his vision for their lives, and enabling lives to be spiritually transformed.

Consider this the *default vision,* a description of the all-purpose ends that any situational leader would be well advised to seek in any situation.

Setting Objectives

With that in mind, and in light of the admonition to become conversant with the fundamentals of leadership, here is my advice if you are a situational leader and want to improve your ability to lead.

- *First, start to think about your world from the vantage point of leadership opportunities.* Try to become more sensitive to the conditions in which you may be expected to provide leadership.

- *Second, to maximize those opportunities for impact, try your best to understand how the head and heart of leaders work:* how they perceive reality, how they think, and how they respond in decision-making situations.
- *Finally, devote some time and energy to becoming an adequate practitioner of core leadership competencies.* You need not master all of these skills and techniques, but you ought to have a basic comprehension of and facility with the more important skills.

Remember, your objective is not to become the world's greatest leader; it is to provide adequate leadership that will help people to get through challenging moments so that they may respond to the mezzo- and macro-level leadership efforts of habitual leaders.

ROLL UP YOUR SLEEVES

Here's what this regimen might look like, in very practical terms. To become more sensitive to leadership situations, realize that leaders respond to particular types of conditions.

First, leaders look for problems that hinder growth or positive change. Their goal is always to facilitate transformation, so solving the barriers that preclude such movement is a key leadership concern. (Leaders deem a problem to be an opportunity in disguise.)

Second, leaders search for indicators that potential is being squandered through inadequate performance. As Christians we are called to do everything with excellence, as if we are doing it for God himself. Leaders, then, identify circumstances in which less-than-superior performance is limiting us and they attempt to enhance the quality with which we perform our tasks.

Third, leaders identify untapped opportunities, seeking new and innovative means of expanding our limits.

A FISH OUT OF WATER

Consider, Confirm, Connect, Conclude, and Consummate

Once you start viewing daily events through this lens, life will look very different—and much more challenging! But you don't want to stop at the point of recognizing opportunities to lead; you need to lead. To do so, follow this five-step process that will set you up for success. You should

- *consider* the situation carefully,
- *confirm* your understanding of it,
- *connect* with relevant people who will affect or be affected by the outcome,
- draw *conclusions* about the best moves to make, and
- *consummate* the process by implementing your course of action.

Consider, confirm, connect, conclude, and consummate. This is a process; it does not come easily, and it does not come immediately.

Practicing the Process

To increase your capability as a situational leader, practice asking yourself some key questions throughout the day regarding the situations in which you find yourself. Is there a leader present? If not, is there a situation in progress that demands focused leadership—that is, someone who will motivate, mobilize, resource, and direct people to act in concert with God's vision? If so, then move through the continuum described above.

Consider the situation carefully, analyzing what's going on, where things are headed, and how they could be enhanced by leadership. Communicate with the others involved in the situation to *confirm* your viewpoint and some of the concerns you are sensing. To *connect* effectively, incorporate the ideas and experiences of those people in your reflections. You may also wish to instigate another form of connection at that point: inviting a habitual leader to assist if the process merits his or her involvement. The habitual leader might be called upon to offer advice or to jump in and lead.

If you determine that it is best for you to rise up and offer situational leadership, then start to *draw some conclusions* about what can be done. Once you decide which *course of action* represents the most beneficial response, go for it! Integrate others into the implementation process. Then stand back and thank God that he was able to use you in a leadership role—even though that is not your primary calling in his service.

If it seems like I glossed over the *draw conclusions* and *consummate* steps, let me take them a level deeper. There are three significant elements in the process.

Before you can draw your conclusions, you must arrive at some bottom-line interpretation of the information you've collected. There's the meaningful difference between data analysis *(this is what we found out; the information says this about the situation)* and data interpretation *(based on that information, here are the implications for the present and future)*. Unless you identify how the data affect people and conditions, you will not be able to draw appropriate conclusions and take transformative action. Spend quality time thinking through the information so that you have a clear perspective on the real conditions.

With that insight in mind, it's time to engage in some basic strategic thinking. The information should help you craft a specific definition of the problem, inefficiency, or opportunity that you are facing. Next, take things to the extreme and describe the optimal outcome or conditions that you would like to see emerge. Then you need to be creative and spell out the different options that you could pursue to get to the optimal condition. In your mind or in discussion or on paper, play out those options to their logical conclusion to determine which scenario offers the best prospects for advancement. Identify it and then sell it to your following.

You sell it by communicating your perspective (problem, possibilities, solution); helping people to see the benefits inherent in your proposed action and the role that each of them will play in making it happen; and jointly determining how to take the next steps.

Leadership Skills for a Lifetime

Does that sound like a lot of work? Good, because leadership is hard work—but it pays great dividends. Does it sound too complex for you? Chances are good that the breaking down of the process makes it seem more expansive and difficult than it needs to be. Honestly, most leaders could not articulate how they lead—it comes naturally to them, so they just do it, almost as a reflex reaction. But if you are not a habitual leader, this type of behavior does not come naturally, so understanding the components of the process is imperative.

This may never become your favorite pastime or a natural response, but you can train yourself to rise to the occasion when necessary and do a creditable job. The more you practice intentional leadership, the easier it will come to you and the more reflexive it will become. Just like learning how to negotiate contracts effectively, discipline your child successfully, communicate complex information with clarity, or manage your household budget, this process takes time to develop.

Since you will be called upon to provide situational leadership for the rest of your life—in places, situations, and at times no one can predict—it is in your best interests (and that of those whom you will be leading) to develop this ability.

How Heather Could Have Responded

Remember how Heather responded to her son's playground brawl? There is no perfect way for her or anyone else to have responded, but it seems obvious that she could have responded more effectively than she did. Leaders do not deny reality; they confront and shape it. She did what came natural to her in that situation, but relying on her inclinations and instincts was not her optimal choice. Even her worst efforts at intentional situational leadership would most likely have generated a better outcome than her leadership-avoidance behavior.

She could have modeled for her son how a believer ideally interacts with other believers when conflict occurs. Without having to be a master negotiator

or hard-nosed agent for her child, she could have worked with the school principal to convene a meeting of all the parties involved in the incident. Once
together, without being offensive or overbearing, Heather could have raised
questions regarding:

- how such an incident could have occurred at a Christian school—and
  what it will take to prevent such outbursts in the future,
- how adequately the teachers on the scene handled the incident—and
  whether the school's faculty needs additional training on how to handle
  such incidents, and
- how well the principal handled the situation in terms of using his authority to seize a "teaching moment" and to impress upon the boys the
  Christian values involved in their handling of the dispute.

(Let me point out that I do not wish to unfairly single out Heather. There
were at least five other adults significantly involved in the situation: the bully's
parents, the school principal, and two teachers. In fact, it was the job of the principal to provide such leadership; his failure to do so raised the necessity for
Heather and Bob to compensate.)

You are who God made you—and there is no reason to change or rue that
nature. But you will encounter times when you must rise up to an occasion and provide leadership, even though God did not design you to be a habitual leader. The
more prepared you are for such moments, the more God will be able to use you in
your areas of skill and passion—even though leadership may not be one of them.

UNCOMFORTABLE QUESTIONS

- Are you a habitual leader or a situational leader?
- What exercises and practices do you intentionally engage in to enhance the
  quality of your leadership?
- Whom do you study to better understand leadership and see how you
  might adapt your natural inclinations to a higher standard of leadership?

- When was the last time you directly asked two or three close friends to give you a completely honest assessment of how you lead in times that demand leadership?
- What did you do about the insights they gave you?

—3—

Leadership on any team should be plural, not singular.

—MIKE KRZYZEWSKI, *Duke University*

Chapter Three

Leadership Is a Team Sport

Ａfter three years as a youth pastor and four years as an assistant pastor, Steve was called to the senior pastorate of a midsized church in the Southeast. He spent hours interacting with people from the church before accepting the position. Steve was excited about it and expected it to be the fulfillment of his lifelong dream: to follow in the footsteps of his father, a senior pastor, serving people through the local church and participating in the transformation of people's lives.

Once on board, Steve began to do what he had been preparing for all his life. He began to forge a bold program for growth at his new ministry outpost, leaning on his seminary training and his observations of what his dad had done in two pastorates a quarter-century earlier. He also remembered the exhortations he had received from the senior pastors he had served under and drew on principles gleaned from conferences, books, and personal discussions. He threw himself into all the varied duties that senior pastors are expected to master, from preaching and leading elders' meetings to baptizing, marrying, confirming, and burying people.

A FISH OUT OF WATER

Steve's honeymoon with the congregation lasted just over a half-year. Around that time people's enthusiasm levels began to wane noticeably. Steve did not disappoint them in some regards. He was, as expected, a capable Bible expositor, a powerful motivational speaker, a good conceptual thinker, and a consistent promoter of the ministry's vision.

Yet time progressed but the church didn't. The people had "been there, done that" before: watching a pastor attempt to be a one-man show. Like his predecessors—and, as some congregants wryly noted, just like the pastors of other churches they had attended in the past—Steve lacked skills in various areas of leadership.

For instance, he was not good at developing the organization needed to fulfill the vision; structures, policies, procedures, and systems were foreign to him. People were pleased at his ability to teach the Scriptures but were disheartened to find him a mediocre strategic thinker; when discussing the vision, he delivered grand themes compellingly but seemed incapable or disinterested when it came time to "put feet" on his lofty ideals. Some congregants noted that this might have been due to his disinclination to gather all the information necessary to make optimal decisions. A widespread complaint was how little time and energy he invested in relationships with key lay leaders and potential leaders. He was clearly more interested in speaking about the long-term goals of the church and getting people excited about those prospects than he was in training the leaders it would take to get there and building leadership teams that would facilitate superior ministry.

In other words, Steve saw the senior pastorate the same way his father, his seminary professors, and his supervising pastors had seen it. It was an outlet for his gifts and talents, with little thought or energy devoted to working with others to build on his strengths and compensate for his weaknesses. As long as he was doing what he did best, and doing it to the best of his ability, he saw no problems with his ministry. God in his sovereignty would bring in the people he needed to cover the gaps in Steve's skill set. In fact, Steve viewed the spreading disenchantment over his limitations as evidence of America's cultural demise. "We have become a nation of critical consumers impatient with things that are not exactly as we want them at any given moment," he preached.

THE ONE-SIZE-FITS-ALL LEADER

As difficult as Steve's current condition may be, he is miles ahead of most pastors and millions of people who hold leadership positions in other organizations. Fortunately, Steve is a habitual leader. Serving in a leadership position works for Steve. Unfortunately, his approach to leadership doesn't.

Steve is hindered by the crippling misconception—one shared by most leaders in America—that because he is the central leader in his organization, everything depends upon him. Sadly, the result is the transfer of knowledge without focused response, well-intended but misguided effort that generates mounting frustration, and idealistic programs that fail to produce lasting results. Steve's approach creates a context in which he is using all of his energy and skills to do everything the best he can. In spite of good intentions and laudable effort, his leadership—like that of every individual leader—leaves much to be desired in the quality and quantity of results.

God cautioned us about the "I must do it all" mentality. Moses was a bright, energetic, competent leader. Yet, in Numbers 18 we read about the horror that his father-in-law Jethro experienced watching Moses try to solve everyone's problems. Moses was working long, difficult days and was becoming physically, emotionally, and spiritually drained by the unending string of needs and expectations of the people. Jethro outlined a plan through which Moses could make the most of his own unique abilities while better addressing people's needs and allowing other gifted leaders to use their skills to contribute to the cause.

Jethro had stumbled onto a key leadership principle: No single individual, even when called and gifted by God to serve as a leader, has all of the resources and abilities required to satisfy the leadership needs of a group. I believe this is because God does not want us thinking that we are indispensable to his kingdom. He loves us and wants us to enjoy using the gifts and abilities he has entrusted to us, but he also wants us to rely upon him for strength and guidance and to acknowledge that all good things we have come from him. Have you ever met or observed a leader whom people described as thinking he was "God's gift to the world"?

God wants us to find joy through our work and the application of our talents, but he does not want us taking sole credit for it. Just as he has made each of us spiritually, physically, emotionally, and intellectually incomplete, so has he rendered all leaders incomplete in their ability to effectively lead people toward God's vision. There is no leader alive who possesses all the gifts, skills, and abilities required to satisfy the entire parcel of leadership needs of any group of people or to do everything necessary to help a group fulfill God's vision for the group.

> *The graveyards are full of indispensable men.*
> —CHARLES DEGAULLE

EVERY LEADER HAS A LEADERSHIP APTITUDE

Early in my career I bought the party line, believing that if leaders work both hard and smart they can do whatever is required to be effective and usher in the fulfillment of the vision. Several years into my research with churches and leaders, though, I was perplexed. The pastors I had known and studied were good people: highly educated, lovers of Christ, honored to serve God, hard workers, well intentioned. Yet, few seemed to be experiencing the kind of results they believed God had called them to pursue.

Addressing this strange reality from several angles, I eventually discovered several reasons that many leaders see such limited results. One explanation was that many people who have leadership positions are not habitual leaders but situational leaders and are therefore fish out of water. (This is the challenge discussed in chapter 2.) A second explanation—germane to our discussion in this chapter—was that every leader has an incomplete set of tools to lead with and must, therefore, know what he can and cannot do. The third bit of wisdom was that effective leaders overcome their weaknesses by combining forces with other leaders whose strengths compensate for those weaknesses, thereby creating a more complete and powerful mix of gifts and abilities.

Taken together, this trio of insights provided a simple but profound explanation of the limitations and failures of so many churches, parachurch ministries, businesses, and nonprofit agencies.

A Discovery of Four Types

My research organization and I discovered there are four types of leaders. We learned that every leader has one of four leadership aptitudes—that is, a relatively predictable set of abilities and perspectives that enables the leader to deliver one dimension of leadership with excellence. A leadership aptitude is not a style of leading as much as it is a person's tendencies and dominant strengths in their leadership efforts.

I also found that every leader—with just a very, very few exceptions—possesses just one leadership aptitude. This is a critical insight because it means that a group will receive complete, effective leadership only when it has multiple leaders whose aptitudes are complementary. The implication, of course, is that leadership is not a solo sport but a team sport.

COMING TO GRIPS WITH YOUR APTITUDE

Understanding your leadership aptitude, then, is vitally important. Such an understanding enables you to determine where and how to focus your efforts. It emphasizes your need to partner with other leaders and helps identify the types of leaders with whom you will become most productive. It underscores the notion that you cannot be the ideal leader that others are seeking. If you are serious about providing effective leadership, these insights will redefine your corporate focus and personal expectations.

Can-Do Attitude Cannot Do It All

Do you expect a man to give birth to a baby? He was part of the conception team, but at this point it is physically impossible for a man to carry the child and physically give birth to that infant. A person with an IQ of eighty whose lifelong dream is to develop the cure for cancer is not going to accomplish that dream; he simply does not have what it takes to arrive at the desired end point. That's analogous to the situation regarding leadership aptitudes: You cannot assign someone to a dimension of leadership for which he is not equipped and expect him to carry it out despite his title, training, desire, and effort.

It is hard for Americans to accept the fact that we cannot do whatever we put our minds to. Leaders, especially, struggle with this because their demeanor is built on self-confidence and a positive, can-do attitude. However, that does not change the fact that you do not determine your leadership aptitude. It was God who called you to be a leader. He chose your leadership aptitude and you cannot do anything about it—nor should you want to, since it's the approach to leadership that will deliver the greatest joy and fulfillment to you and the people whom he allows you to lead.

Are you a leader? If so, then get used to the fact that you are one of four types of leaders we will discuss: directing, strategic, team-building, or operational.

What Leads to Misunderstanding Aptitudes

We're talking about these four leadership aptitudes as dominant. You will not be completely bereft of the abilities that are the primary focus of other aptitudes. On the other hand, sometimes we misunderstand our aptitudes or assume that we have multiple leadership aptitudes because we have had to act like a multiple-aptitude leader in the absence of partners who possess aptitudes that complement our dominant capacity. Sometimes we confuse leadership aptitude and personal style. We fail to realize that an aptitude transcends mere style because it reflects a mixture of personality, thinking style, and approach to using information, giftedness, and emotional response—things that make you who you are and that you are generally powerless to change.

Your aptitude reflects your innate identity and capacity. The more you can honestly comprehend those strengths and weaknesses, the better you will realize the tremendous value your aptitude provides to those whom you lead—and how utterly incapable you are of providing complete leadership.

You may be wondering what your aptitude is and what kind of leaders you need to identify and partner with for greater impact. There are many good tests on the market. One is our Christian Leader Profile, a confidential, self-administered on-line inventory. The results will give you a sense of whether you are a habitual or situational leader, what type of leader you are, and how to strengthen your leadership potential.

THE FOUR APTITUDES DEFINED

Let me describe each of the four types. You will probably identify a number of similarities between how you lead and one of the four aptitudes described below.

The Directing Leaders

When people think about leaders, the type of leader they usually bring to mind is directing leaders. George W. Bush and Ronald Reagan are examples. These leaders excel at conveying a compelling vision. They do not invest much of their energy in the details of the process; you rarely hear of a directing leader who is "a control freak" or who indulges in micromanaging. Instead, these people excite others about the way things could be (by conveying the vision). They enlist people to become part of the solution rather than the problem and to feel good about joining with others to facilitate positive change (in other words, motivate). Directing leaders keep people pumped up, pointed in a specific direction, and hopeful about the future.

Directing leaders create energy around a vision; they are catalysts of change. They excite people's imaginations and enable them to believe in themselves, which in turn draws more people to both the leader and his cause. Directing leaders are effective public speakers and good listeners. They make people feel as if they matter.

One of the core behaviors of leaders is to make decisions on behalf of a group. Over the years I have learned that directing leaders are proficient at making decisions. Although they often have endured numerous meetings and discussions related to a key decision and have sifted through mountains of factual data, directing leaders are often driven by instinct rather than facts.

This tendency is fed by a lifelong track record of success based largely upon their reliance on intuition. Sometimes, as they share their decision with the other leaders in their team, the forceful opposition of their teammates will cause these leaders to abruptly change their mind. This often causes observers to doubt the leader's depth and skill, but the about-face is usually made on the basis of their "feel" for the situation influenced by the arguments, emotions, and other dynamics they sensed among their trusted colleagues.

Directing leaders do not avoid making the tough calls, although sometimes they take longer than others deem necessary. Those delays are often traced to the directing leader's not having a "sense of peace" or clarity about the choices they face. You will find during times of high stress, instability, or uncertainty that the wisdom, courage, and self-confidence of directing leaders soothe the hearts of the average constituent. (The guidance provided by Mayor Rudy Giuliani during the September 11 terrorist crisis was a vivid example.) Directing leaders who are Christians tend to be sensitive to the values and beliefs that drive their worldview and shudder at the notion of compromising their core values. Those values are a necessary touchstone that helps to shape their instincts.

If they sound like complete leaders, let me mention some of their imperfections. Directing leaders have little interest in or patience with the details of the process. They recognize the need for getting the facts and considering all relevant options, but they rarely throw themselves into that process. They tend to be restless, have short attention spans, favor action over reflection, and have been described by fellow leaders as loose cannons. Once they have made their decision, they often lose interest and begin searching for the next challenge to address. They demand assurances that progress is being made with expedience and excellence but are not prone to dive into the minutiae.

These individuals know that structure is important, but they don't much care how it is developed, what it looks like, or what must happen to maintain the structure. They genuinely love people, but they typically cause chaos when they attempt to organize people around the vision, goals, and strategies that they have promoted. Because they are supremely confident in themselves and are sold out to the vision they espouse, they generally ignore financial limitations and realities, believing that if they have adequately sold people on the vision, followers will sacrificially give whatever is required to bring the vision to pass. They possess little appetite for drawn-out in-house debates over procedure and may rudely cut off colleagues in midsentence once they reach their limit. Their interest is in making good things happen—now!

The Strategic Leader

Generally speaking, the classic strategic leader is one who shuns the limelight in favor of gathering and analyzing mountains of data with which to make the best possible choices. These people enjoy the intellectual gamesmanship of crafting possible scenarios and conceptually playing them out to their logical extreme, resulting in recommendations as to the optimal alternative. They enjoy laboring over detailed plans to make sure all of the bases are covered and that the vision will become a reality. Again leaning on the political world for an archetype, Al Gore is an example of the strategic leader.

Strategic leaders are not vision conceivers and communicators as much as they are vision developers and shapers. Their contribution to the pursuit of the vision is creating practical means of turning a compelling idea of a preferable future into a viable plan of action to make that future a reality. They make that contribution by painstakingly scrutinizing reality—people, organizations, situations, ideas, activity—to draw conclusions that will help them facilitate the vision. They tend to be quite thorough in their explorations—much to the chagrin of the impatient directing leader and to the perplexity of the next leader we will meet, the team-building leader who struggles to understand the process and the payoff. They do not hesitate to ask the hard questions. They don't mind creating controversy because their primary quest is to understand reality so that they can develop a workable plan. Once they have the pertinent facts and have carefully analyzed them, strategic leaders are prone to developing creative, albeit sometimes complex, solutions.

Strategic leaders usually take great pride in their preparation and the resulting level of expertise they achieve. It is rare to find a strategic leader who is at a loss to explain something; however, if they do not know the answer, such a deficiency fuels their zest for further discovery. Strategic leaders almost always overprepare for meetings. Should you ask them a question, you are likely to get more detail than you care to hear—unless, of course, you, too, are a strategic leader. They have a tendency toward perfectionism, which often causes them to miss (or at least complain about) deadlines.

Don't expect your strategic leaders to get the masses cheering and clamoring for action; they're more likely to skip the public rallies than to lead them. This is because strategic leaders are not driven by emotion; in fact, emotion is seen as a sign of weakness or intellectual inferiority in their eyes. They understand the value of getting people emotionally jazzed, but it's not a style that energizes them. That very detachment, however, is one of their greatest strengths, since it enables them to develop objective conclusions. They are more likely to view people's emotions as something to be exploited than something to be valued.

In the end, strategic leaders maintain firm allegiance to truth and efficiency. They believe these factors are instrumental toward converting vision into reality. In fact, they are more loyal to the vision than they are to people. Their focus on facts, figures, plans, and possibilities routinely leads others to portray them as insensitive, unemotional, or even robotic. Although they have feelings and care for people, they have a deep-seated mistrust of feelings—and, often, of people. Strategic leaders are usually deemed to be significant contributors to the team but are often the "forgotten" member of the leadership team. They are rarely the most popular leader on a team. Not surprisingly, this does not phase them; they are generally happier working with ideas than with people.

A common complaint about strategic leaders is that they take so long to arrive at decisions. This is frequently because they refuse to make decisions until they feel they have mined all the data that exists for clues and have had ample time to consider all reasonable possibilities and implications. These are people who believe they can eliminate all risks in decision making if they can just analyze enough data. Of course, nobody ever gets that much data, but the inclination means that strategic leaders are risk-averse.

Strategic leaders are capable of juggling many details, but they deal better with conceptual details than organizational details. They understand the "hot buttons" that move people to action but are not emotionally equipped to push those buttons. When they speak publicly they are usually precise, complete, and focused—and long-winded, boring, and lacking the spark that ignites people's enthusiasm. Although they are effective at identifying the kinds of teams and work groups required to make progress, they are generally not the people you'd want recruiting and maintaining those teams.

A Fish Out of Water

No group is likely to succeed at fulfilling God's vision without enabling people to effectively work together. For such unity and cooperation to occur, someone has to identify and pursue the appropriate people, determine their gifts and abilities, knit them into complementary work units, and provide the emotional energy that keeps them going. That's the role of the team-building leader. Bill McCartney, of Promise Keepers fame, is a powerful team-building leader using his abilities for God's kingdom today.

Directing leaders love the chase. Strategic leaders love the mind games involved in mapping out the chase. We'll meet operational leaders in a minute, who enjoy managing the resources that allow the chase to be consummated. Team-building leaders are enamored of the interactive dimension of the chase.

Team-building leaders see the pursuit of the vision as a giant puzzle in which every person they meet is a piece searching for his or her appropriate place. The team builder's role is to help them find, enjoy, and succeed in that place.

These leaders blend vision and personal ability by organizing people around a common cause. Inveterate networkers, they bring together people with a shared interest in specific outcomes related to the vision and nurture those interests into a full-blown passion for the team and its vision. Being with people energizes them, and people are energized by their presence; team builders generally have an upbeat personality, optimistic perspective, and encouraging demeanor. After spending time with a team-building leader you most likely feel as if you have been heard, understood, and loved by a trusted friend.

As people-savvy leaders, these types exploit their charisma and popularity to motivate people to get involved and to give it their best shot. By focusing on matching people's abilities with the tasks at hand and with people who possess complementary abilities these leaders develop a number of effective work groups and coalitions that produce significant, vision-related outcomes.

Team-building leaders are upbeat and lovable—until it comes time to sit through meetings, turn in paperwork, or read internal memos. The stories are legion of team builders who unwittingly undermined well-constructed plans by simply ignoring anything that was put on paper—work assignments, legal cautions, action plans, operational budgets, or other directives. In fact, team-building leaders have a tendency to waffle on details, too.

Unless they are very careful, team builders can also be victimized by their greatest strength—relationships—by investing too much trust and confidence in people who do not (or, sometimes, cannot) pull through as promised. While directing and strategic leaders may burn out, team builders more often get burned. Their inattention to structure or to resource management sometimes burns people, too. A true partnership with leaders who possess complementary aptitudes can boost the effectiveness of team builders—and their organization—tremendously.

The Operational Leader

Given a trio that is good with ideas, information, and people, the missing link to effectiveness is someone who masters process. That's exactly what operational leaders bring to the mix. Their forte is leading people by developing systems around the vision, resources, and opportunities available, creating new routines that maximize whatever they have to work with, in light of where they want to go.

Directing leaders excel at creating dissonance to facilitate change. Strategic leaders add value by crafting a persuasive case for a given direction. Team builders get the horses in place and moving in unison. Operational leaders build the systems that tie everyone's contributions together. Their efforts provide stability, predictability, and consistency—all qualities that strengthen not only the leadership team but also the efforts of the organization as it moves toward the fulfillment of the vision.

There is a significant and clear distinction that must be made between leaders and managers. Whereas managers tend to maintain and improve upon what exists, operational leaders create new opportunities and solutions that result in breakthroughs. In other words, they conceive and introduce new routines designed to facilitate the accomplishment of the vision.

Operational leaders may be well-liked, but they are usually low-key and low profile. They devise systems that make things run smoothly—and, in the wake of the chaos and roadblocks generated by the other three types of leaders, a structural architect is needed to enable ministry to flow efficiently. These leaders are somewhat chameleonlike in their duties: they initiate, coordinate, integrate, facilitate, evaluate, and enhance people's efforts. Their enemies are inefficiency, loose ends, communications breakdowns, cost-overruns, missed deadlines, and legal crises. They are very concrete thinkers and devote their time to the kinds of practical details that the other three types ignore but which will make or break the organization's vision drive.

By focusing on operational details every day, the operational leader sometimes behaves more like a manager than a leader, championing the mechanics of a system rather than the purpose of those mechanics—in other words, to facilitate making the vision a reality. That confusion can seriously impair the ministry; without anyone tending to the financial, administrative, or systemic needs of the organization, required correctives may be overlooked.

These leaders, by nature, dislike conflict. To avoid emotional tugs-of-war they may surrender too easily. To maintain momentum and energy, they may avoid delivering bad news. Often, other leaders must listen carefully to subtle clues that the operational leader drops regarding current or coming crises; not wishing to be the bearer of bad news, they downplay the realities and hope that things will work out for the best.

POTENTIAL DISASTERS

Organizations often encourage people to work with the individuals with whom they feel most comfortable. This tendency is fraught with danger, however, because we typically prefer working alongside people just like ourselves since they agree with our views, care about the same things we do, and don't obsess on things we aren't passionate about. Consequently, there is an inclination for directing leaders to attract and appoint other directing leaders to the inner circle, just as strategic, team-building, and operational leaders also gravitate to their own kind. After all, we feel most deeply affirmed and accepted when we're around people who are most like us.

But our research shows that this tendency can be destructive. What seems like a perfect match designed to make us feel comfortable and productive usually winds up producing distress and disaster. Although there is a significant learning curve involved, working intimately with leaders who have different aptitudes multiplies our efforts in ways we would never experience otherwise.

Because of substantially different approaches to dealing with the same situation, a team of leaders with divergent aptitudes will experience times of discomfort and instances of misunderstanding. Let's call it creative tension. But when that tension is intelligently and strategically managed, it can push a team to greater heights of productivity, innovation, and unity. In fact, we've found that when that tension is removed you eliminate one of the strengths of the team.

Too Much of a Good Thing

Take it even a step further. Based on the descriptions of the leader types provided above, think about the dynamics of having four directing leaders trying to work together on the same team. It would be like having a basketball team with five shooting guards on the floor at the same time: lots of ability, range, and desire, but not enough balls to go around! Each of the directing leaders would naturally want to lead the process, have the stage to communicate the key details to people, feel the pressure—and exhilaration—of making tough choices, and experience the challenge of getting people to understand and embrace the vision. But who would do the homework to figure out which options make the most sense? Who would coordinate the activities of those who sign on for the challenge, whether employees or volunteers? Who would develop a process to enable things to run smoothly?

Would it be any better if you had four strategic leaders melded together into a team? Not really. Although they disdain the spotlight and have fewer relational needs than others do, this group would be a toxic mix. Granted, you would have a world-class information base, insightful analysis, brilliant scenarios, minute documentation, and terrific plans. But who would persuade people to follow this group? Who would keep them on track? Who would develop the resources required to pull off their complex ideas?

Since the difficulties enumerated thus far often relate to people skills, perhaps a quartet of team-building leaders would make sense. Alas, this group would have the most fun meetings, raise people's spirits through the roof, and create a network of people unsurpassed. But to what end? Without the skills provided by the other leaders, those associated with this quartet would suffer from vision drift, absence of resources, unwise strategy, inefficient procedures, and running over budget and behind schedule.

Blending a handful of operational leaders would result in efficient meetings, streamlined administrative practices, detailed job descriptions, and a paper trail a mile long. But would anyone be inspired to jump on board? Where would the resource base come from? Who would decide which options should prevail or how to organize a contingent of available human resources?

Thus the conclusion to draw is that merely piecing together a group of warm bodies who are capable of working together—even if they agree on specific outcomes—is not likely to produce optimal results. Teams work best when they are comprised of individuals whose personal abilities and gifts contribute value, while their personal deficiencies are compensated for via the abilities and efforts of other team members.

Leadership Is a Team Sport

Paying Attention to the Other Aptitudes

Approaching this matter differently, though, we can realize that every leader has some ability in areas outside his or her dominant aptitude. Identifying and focusing upon your area of strength does not excuse you from doing what must be done in a situation because it's not your primary focus.

For instance, a directing leader should not ignore the financial realities of a decision simply because he is not as competent a financial analyst as the team's operational leader. A strategic leader must sometimes mobilize people around a task, even though a team-building leader is likely to be more adept at it and the strategic leader may loathe doing it. Team builders cannot refuse to work in concert with a strategic plan simply because they are not naturally inclined to plan and to work within such guidelines. Operational leaders cannot be excused for refusing to keep coworkers focused on the vision, even though continually articulating that theme is the primary purview of the directing leader.

If you are to lead people, you must do what it takes to get the job done as well as it can be done—which typically means teaming with other gifted leaders whose abilities complement yours. Knowing your aptitude and working within a team environment are practices that facilitate an optimal exercise of leadership, but it will not create a perfect experience.

THE ULTIMATE COMBINATION

Think about Pastor Steve and the millions of pastors, business executives, government officials, and family leaders who strive to do all aspects of leadership for their respective constituencies. How personally and corporately debilitating it is for one individual to try to be the answer to everyone's problem and to be the sole means through which people experience God's plan on earth! Doesn't it make you tired just thinking about it?

A FISH OUT OF WATER

A Dream Team

Now pause for a moment and imagine the power of a quartet in which each individual is a leader—called by God, possessing Christlike character, and capable of carrying out necessary tasks to move people toward the vision—and fills in the gaps left by each of the others. As a leader, have you had the benefit of serving alongside a trio of individuals whose combination of abilities allows you to pour yourself into those aspects of leadership that you enjoy, that you do well, and about which you are most passionate? Can you understand how joining these four types of leaders together would give rise to a dynamic, multifaceted hub of wisdom, experience, capabilities, and empowerment?

Clearly, the contribution of each of these individuals is indispensable. Just as surely, no person alive could possibly encompass all the perspectives, experiences, education, skills, and gifts demanded to represent all of these aptitudes. In fact, we find it the incredibly rare individual who possesses two aptitudes.

> *Never let a person's weakness get in the way of his strength.*
> —**MIKE KRYZEWSKI,** *Duke University*

If you are a leader, you must determine which one of these aptitudes you harbor—and how to utilize your aptitude in concert with others who possess a passion for the same godly vision yet operate with a different aptitude.

The Inevitability of Conflict

Be prepared, however, for some rough sailing within each leadership team involved in your organization. Because each leader type approaches the same situation differently—unique ways of perceiving, analyzing, responding, and evaluating—tension within the team is inevitable.

There are two types of tension, though: constructive and destructive. Constructive tension is that which enables each leader to push coleaders toward the most complete and effective action, adding what he or she uniquely understands to the contributions of fellow leaders. Destructive tension is that caused by ego, inflexibility, and selfishness.

Constructive tension is natural and beneficial. The philosophy underlying leadership teams suggests that four heads are better than one and that each head must contribute something different to the final mix. Thus, tension is to be expected if each leader is solving problems and exploiting opportunities from a different angle. The shared vision is the element that unites them.

There are insights that may help you to maximize each leader's contribution and reduce the tendency to challenge what others offer. Here are some observations from my research with leadership teams that may help minimize misunderstanding and unproductive conflict within the team.

What Directing Leaders Need

Get used to listening to directing leaders talk; they often arrive at conclusions by verbalizing the thoughts running through their minds until they talk themselves into a decision. This particularly disturbs strategic leaders, who cherish accuracy and economy of communication. Paradoxically, directors are impatient with others who do the same thing, so tension is minimized when colleagues state their case short and sweet. Although they have a tendency to overschedule themselves, directing leaders also struggle with time limits.

These leaders need team members to relate their plans and ideas back to the vision and values of the organization; those are the touchstones of directors. If you are convinced that the director is moving in the wrong direction, present your case with persuasive facts and personal passion. Do not attack directors personally, and always anchor your remarks to the vision and values. Increase the chance of gaining their support by making factual statements followed by clarifying questions. They are also more likely to get onboard with a different approach when they feel they have been instrumental in arriving at that conclusion.

A FISH OUT OF WATER

What Strategic Leaders Need

Being right is of ultimate importance to these leaders. If you are convinced they are barking up the wrong tree, keep your feelings out of the discussion; that will merely solidify their determination to argue you into accepting their point of view. Instead, marshal a convincing case based on facts. These individuals respond well to genuine and deserved compliments—and build a lasting distrust of people who give superficial, inauthentic compliments. Time matters to these leaders, so use their time carefully; they tend to avoid those who brazenly waste or inefficiently use time.

Strategic leaders are comfortable with people seizing their ideas and expanding them to gain greater acceptance and impact. They do, however, need some acknowledgment for providing the foundational concept. Their perfectionism undermines their value to the organization; tying their expectations and rewards to timely performance increases their value to the team effort. Be prepared to regularly remind them of pending deadlines and the importance of conforming to the calendar.

What Team-Building Leaders Need

These people are smart, but they are more likely to be moved by emotion than reason. Often, they will support a plan simply because a person they like and trust is promoting it; they believe in the character of people more than infallibility of content. Gaining their help, then, requires some hand-holding. Be sure to make them feel welcomed and involved before jumping into a factual presentation; they won't get into the flow of the conversation until some heart has been shown. They do poorly with one-way communication (in other words, lectures); they won't own a process until they have had a chance to interact with the presenter.

Gaining the involvement of team builders means stressing the emotional benefits of the proposed courses of action and reiterating the importance of the people who will be involved. Because they unconsciously serve as the defenders of those people whom they lead, they protect followers from exploitation and being taken for granted. They serve as the gatekeepers to the troops. Open the gate by acknowledging the value of those people.

Team builders have a tendency to lose their focus unless there is a firm, clear depiction of what is expected and the parameters within which such action must be taken. They can handle discussions of multiple options, but they do their best work when there is an unambiguous definition of the final choice.

What Operational Leaders Need

Always balancing leadership and management, these people do their best work when they have a clear comprehension of the bottom-line priorities and the freedom to create a framework for success. Priorities can be difficult for them to determine; they sometimes fall into the trap of thinking that all progress is of equal importance, that maintaining forward movement is ample evidence of effectiveness. Helping these individuals recognize relative priorities and to have a clear sense of limitations and parameters will put them at ease and maximize their contribution. Having them regularly interact with coleaders who are more certain of the comparative significance of various efforts and outcomes is invaluable.

Occasionally these leaders are loath to let go of a system, policy, or procedure they developed, even though it has outlived its utility. Walking them through the need to do so and supporting them in the process itself pays dividends. Similarly, coaching them through confrontational episodes with others is often necessary to facilitate the emotionally wrenching meetings that must take place to move the organization forward. Complimenting them on their courage and performance after such confrontations paves the way toward greater comfort with future conflict situations.

But let's take this discussion even further. I have alluded to maximizing your impact by working within a team comprised of leaders whose aptitudes are distinct from yours. Let's briefly discuss the process of developing such a team.

A Fish Out of Water

Building Aptitude-Sensitive Teams

Teams are incredibly powerful leadership structures. As one leader explained to me, "A team always outperforms an individual. The more you are able to bring together leaders whose skills and training builds upon what the others bring, the greater the ultimate outcome of their cooperative effort."

Just as Moses, Joshua, David, Paul, Nehemiah, Joseph, and many other great leaders in Scripture—including Jesus Christ—led within a team-based model, so should we strive to create the most efficient and effective team of leaders who share a common vision from God.

The ideal team is comprised of four leaders, each representing a different aptitude. In fact, we have seen time after time that the absence of any one of the four aptitudes renders the ministry vulnerable and unstable. A team that

> *Even if you have a sense of what's around the corner, if you don't have a team in place that can execute your plan, there's a big problem.*
> —STEPHEN CASE, *AOL Time Warner*

blends these four aptitudes is one that has the potential to accomplish great things for the kingdom, with excellence, efficacy, and efficiency.

Not a Committee

Realize that the leadership team is not merely a work group—a collection of people who are brought together to accomplish specific tasks under the direction of a leader. Nor is it a committee—since a leadership team has decision-making authority, is composed of individuals called by God rather than appointed by people, and is committed to pursuing vision rather than simply researching, discussing, or recommending action regarding a specific issue.

Your leadership team may have more than four people because the time commitment required exceeds what certain leaders (for example, volunteer leaders in a church or nonprofit organization) are able to devote to the process, causing them to split or share a dimension of leadership with a similarly gifted leader.

Where to Find Them

One of the barriers to leaders seeking to develop a team is the assumption that God has failed to provide the mix of leaders necessary to develop a viable team. Sometimes the lack is there, necessitating a focused search and recruitment process. But more often it seems that God has provided the people needed, but those individuals have not been linked for impact.

In practical terms, how do you find coleaders whose aptitudes complement yours?

Certainly you need to know what kind of leader you are—that's the best starting point so that you do not wind up joined with leaders who possess your aptitude. Armed with that knowledge, identify all of the leaders involved in your organization and their dominant leadership aptitude. In relation to each leader check to see if they have a "team spirit"—that is, a willingness and capability of working with others rather than in isolation. That capacity is evidenced by being teachable, having spiritual maturity, perceiving leadership to be an act of servanthood, having passion for the vision and for leading people toward it, and having a sufficient skill level (or the potential to get to that level in a reasonable time) that would enable them to add value to the team.

Every organization that grows in size and function develops multiple leadership teams. Determining who is best poised to be on which team is determined by the individual's personal vision and passion, leadership maturity, aptitude, and interpersonal chemistry. The good news for leaders is that there is always more demand than supply, but that means we also have to be careful that we accept responsibilities that truly fit who we are and where we have been called by God to serve.

A Fish Out of Water

Another observation from my work with leaders is that they sometimes set themselves up for hardship by venturing too far into the domain of aptitudes that they do not possess. Let me give a few examples of how you have probably experienced this practice of "aptitude expansion" that disables the leader and hurts the organization.

Micromanaging

In an attempt to make sure things are being done properly, you sometimes get a directing, strategic, or team-building leader who devotes too much time and energy to tracking down, scrutinizing, and responding to details of projects that they have no business examining.

Naturally, a healthy balance is called for in their work: All leaders make decisions and should base their choices on reasonable assumptions and reliable information. Spending too much time and energy digging into the fact base, though, slows down the organization, diverts the leader's attention and impact, and both confuses and extinguishes the enthusiasm of people. Leaders guilty of such inappropriate tinkering are undermining their own ability to focus on delivering what they uniquely offer to the organization while discouraging others who are seeking to help. This condition has come to be known as micromanaging. While an obsession on details is the rightful domain of operational leaders, this penchant becomes a significant and widespread dilemma that other types of leaders must recognize about themselves and overcome.

Overselling the Vision

In some situations you will find the strategic, team-building, and operational leaders devoting way too much of their resources to articulating the vision for people. Although every leader's starting point for activity must be a clear understanding and ownership of the vision, and must develop whatever he or she does around that vision, some leaders of the three types identified above get stuck on that aspect and thus fail to devote themselves to the application of the vision from their unique set of skills and abilities. Their constant emphasis on noodling over and discussing the basic vision with people becomes redundant and counterproductive. It is the directing leader's responsibility to keep people focused on the vision; when others perseverate on it, they get labeled theoretical and become marginalized as impractical.

Too Much Data, Not Enough Decision Making

Progress requires that leaders understand their context and have a firm knowledge of the alternatives they could pursue to be both effective and efficient. Helping the leadership team to arrive at such intelligence is the dominant emphasis of strategic leaders. Have you ever been involved in an organization where the other leaders spent so much time collecting information and endlessly discussing it that decisions were never made? Granted, the homework must be done prior to making key decisions, but when multiple leaders cover the same ground it becomes wasteful and competitive. This disease is a version of analysis paralysis: too many leaders investing too many resources in gathering and considering data without getting to the point of decision and application.

Overboard Networking

Perhaps you have encountered situations in which directing, strategic, or operational leaders spent an unusual amount of time networking and trying to enlist the engagement of people in the organization's efforts. While this is certainly a leadership function, and leaders are to be encouraged to spend time with people and to motivate them to get involved, when such attempts become excessive you may hear people start to talk about leadership that is too political. When you start having multiple leaders fawning over individuals in an unrestrained effort to befriend and recruit them, the resulting chaos becomes a turnoff to many individuals and reduces the organization's ability to make headway smoothly.

When you are able to work as a team with leaders who have complementary aptitudes, everyone is best served by focusing on their particular areas of strength. Duplication of effort often produces friction and may lead to the unraveling of an otherwise competent and productive team.

Set Yourself Up for Success

Since his youth, Pastor Steve has been taught that a leader can be all things to all people. He had even heard passages of Scripture, such as I Corinthians 9:19–23, given as a biblical basis for trying to be everyone's solution. That had become his view of leadership—and, in the end, it severely hindered his capacity to build the ministry he had been called to lead.

If you are striving to be the leader around which everything revolves, pray about how you might disabuse yourself of that perspective of leadership in favor of a healthier approach based on maximizing your strengths and compensating for your weaknesses through a team approach.

Christian leaders must keep in mind that when we lead, the focus of our efforts is not us; we lead because we have been called by God to lead by rallying people around a God-given vision. Contrary to what the motivational speakers suggest, none of us has all the skills, energy, ability, and resources to successfully enable God's people to bring his vision to fruition. Instead, be motivated and energized by the realization that you do not have to be all things to all people; you just need to be the powerful, limited, and focused leader whom God created you to be.

Leadership Is a Team Sport

Uncomfortable Questions

- In the organization or group to which you provide leadership, who are the other leaders who complement your own aptitude?
- Who in your leadership mix is guilty of micromanaging, analysis paralysis, theoretical leadership, or politics—and what is the rest of the team doing to prevent future occurrences of the practice?
- Think about the tensions and arguments among you and your teammates recently. Which of those conflicts were the result of constructive tension, and how wisely were those conflicts resolved? Which conflicts resulted from destructive tendencies, and how strategically were they handled?

—4—

> *The reasonable man adapts himself to the world; the unreasonable man persists in trying to adapt the world to himself. Therefore, all progress depends on the unreasonable man.*
>
> —GEORGE BERNARD SHAW

CHAPTER FOUR

What's Your Point?

EW PEOPLE took their work as seriously as Valerie. She had spent twenty-plus years working her way up the corporate ladder in the retail industry while volunteering in ministry at her church. When the director of discipleship left for another church, the senior pastor floored Valerie by asking her to pray about taking the position. After several weeks of fervent prayer, self-doubt, excitement, animated conversations with friends, and lively interviews with the pastors and elders, Valerie accepted the opportunity. With characteristic abandon, she threw herself into her new work.

During her first month on the job the senior pastor spent an hour a day for three days each week interacting with Valerie, driving home the significance of the church's vision and how important it would be for her to run with the vision in the discipleship ministry. She asked a lot of questions, took loads of notes, and had every intention of increasing the effectiveness of the equipping process at the church. In short order she crafted a vision statement for her ministry: "To equip the saints to be more like Jesus."

Throughout her first year on the job Valerie showed that she had leadership skills. She was able to get people excited about the notion of a deeper Christian experience. She aptly delegated authority and responsibility to capable leaders, communicated her ideas and goals clearly, and demonstrated courage and strategic problem-solving abilities. People loved her sense of humor, her humility, and her enthusiasm for developing people's spiritual lives. They could even see positive changes in her own spiritual depth as she committed to practicing what she preached.

Yet in the few moments when she wasn't running hard, Valerie realized that something was missing. She was able to get many people excited, but she couldn't sustain the excitement. Others never got excited in the first place. Publicly she ascribed this to people's lukewarm commitment to the hard work of becoming a true disciple. But inwardly she knew there was something else, something she couldn't put her finger on.

At her first review, the personnel team from the church was well prepared and complimentary. However, the chairman of the committee stopped her in her tracks by telling her that she needed to clarify the vision for the discipleship ministry and focus more tightly on pursuing that vision. Valerie protested that she had been doing so.

"No," the chairman said. "We've talked with a dozen or so people from the congregation who verified our observations. Your department is doing what is traditionally done in discipleship ministries. But it is not vision-based."

She sought to defend her efforts by pointing to the vision statement that she had leaned on throughout the year.

"That's a mission statement, not a vision statement," he said.

The group helped Valerie to see that she was working hard and had the right heart but was devoted to delivering efficient programs and growing numbers of people-satisfied "customers." This was laudable, but it was not related to an organizing concept and motivating passion that provided the church's strategic direction, facilitated the rejection of great but unrelated opportunities, and promoted a laserlike focus on a specific and unique calling.

What's Your Point?

Valerie spent the next few days in virtual isolation, replaying the jolting conversation in her head. She reviewed her first year of activity and her plan for the next two years. It was a full agenda: initiating new programs, training more teachers and mentors, sponsoring developmental events, identifying and making the best resources accessible. Nevertheless, the time spent with the personnel committee had produced a great awakening for Valerie. She realized she did not have a clear sense of God's vision for her ministry.

DOES VISION REALLY MATTER?

Perhaps you have been in a situation like Valerie, where you know you have been called to lead people, you have ample evidence of your gifts and abilities to provide such leadership, and you have thrown yourself wholeheartedly into the process of pursuing goals you have set for your efforts. Yet, after weeks, months, or perhaps even years of hard work you have seen little fruit from your effort. You thought you were pursuing God's vision and even used a "vision statement" in meetings and planning sessions, yet something isn't clicking.

As you run through a checklist of possible blockages to effective leadership, be sure you ascertain the centrality of God's vision for your work. More often than not, leaders in such situations are battling with a vision problem—even when they think they already have dealt with it.

Many high-profile leaders have been hampered by a lack of vision. During his 1992 election campaign, President George H. Bush created a stir by denigrating "the vision thing"—people's ardent desire to know his vision for the nation before they would entrust it to his care. Our research, however, showed that the incumbent chief executive's inability to convey a sense of the future to which he was committed (and committing the nation) was the factor most responsible for his defeat at the hands of his relatively unknown challenger, the vision-laden former governor of Arkansas, Bill Clinton.

Former President Bush is not alone. Other leaders who had the technical skills to make a difference but lacked the fire and focus that vision injects into the process are found in every dimension of life, from business, government, nonprofit activity, and ministry realms to parenting, coaching, small groups, or simply counseling friends and neighbors.

A decade after researching and writing a best-selling book about vision, I am still learning about the dynamics of vision—and how many people embrace the concept but fail to implement it.[1]

What could be worse than being born without sight? Being born with sight and no vision.

—HELEN KELLER

Developing a clear, concise, and compelling vision is hard work. Developing your activity around such vision is a major challenge. But the alternative is to spin your wheels doing the predictable with limited influence and insignificant productivity. God has called you to do more than turn a profit, be kind to others, and participate in congregational life. Those are good endeavors, but they are not the life-changing outcomes to which God is calling you. As a situational or habitual leader you are called to lead people to accomplish something very important within the framework of his grand plan for humanity. Do you know what that is?

DEFINING VISION

Vision is not some mystical, ambiguous, or abstract fantasy. God's vision for his people provides a clear and compelling mental portrait of a preferable future that he conveys to his chosen servants—that is, to his appointed leaders. It is a specific and unique calling to an individual or group that gives particular direction, limitations, and hope. It comes from God. He delivers it to those whom he has called as leaders; it acts as his primary marching orders for those servants. It is meant to be the central, organizing principle and directive of a leader's activity.

Vision, then, is a portrait of a better future that we may participate in developing. It is not a weight to bear or an expectation to struggle under. Through vision God provides us with a foretaste of how he would like to use us in order to receive maximum blessing and joy. In fact, it is the absence of vision that should instill fear and trembling within a leader, for that condition suggests that we are operating on our own skill, wisdom, and creativity in a world beyond our control.

> *If a man hasn't found something he is willing to die for, he isn't fit to live.*
> —MARTIN LUTHER KING JR.

Solomon described the significance of vision succinctly in Proverbs 29:18. The King James Version translates his thought as, "where there is no vision, the people perish." The New International Version amplifies that notion: "Where there is no revelation, the people cast off restraint." The Living Bible lays down the challenge: "Where there is ignorance of God, the people run wild."

Vision and Impact

One of the strongest relationships I have seen in twenty years of research on the topic is this: There is a direct correlation between the impact of an individual or an organization and the presence of God's vision as the driving force behind the activity that brought such influence.

For example, the typical church is a fairly small group of people that convenes weekly and has limited impact on the culture. The typical senior pastor of such a church has no sense of God's vision—in fact, fewer than 10 percent of all Protestant senior pastors in the nation can articulate God's vision for their church. On the other hand, there are several thousand churches in America that are growing both numerically and in relation to influence regarding life change. In more than four out of five of those congregations we find senior pastors who understand, articulate, and energetically champion God's vision with certainty and fervor, producing purposeful centers of blessing and transformation.

The difference is striking—and the lesson is undeniable: God's vision is instrumental and irreplaceable for those who wish to be and do all that God intends.

Four Primary Challenges

In my research I have found four major vision-related obstacles to effective leadership. They are (1) the absence of God's vision, (2) the operative vision not being God's, (3) the foundational vision not being a shared vision, and (4) the vision being peripheral to the development of the enterprise.

Any one of these will impair an organization's striving to have meaningful purpose and lasting positive impact.

Absence of Vision

The most common barrier is that God's vision is altogether absent from the process. Generally this is out of ignorance or ambivalence, although in some cases it is because the organization has equated mission with vision. Sometimes the dismissal of vision is attributable to ignorance of its benefits.

The Blessings of Obedience

Basing your leadership on God's vision is a matter of obedience first and foremost, but such obedience brings with it tangible advantages. Three parties are blessed by the implementation of God's vision: (1) God (who revels in our obedience), (2) the vision champion (a leader committed to seeing the vision fulfilled), and (3) the beneficiaries (namely, the people whose lives are positively affected by the process and product of fulfilling the vision).

Among the benefits received by pursuing and experiencing the completion of the vision are

- a more intense relationship with God, since he reveals the vision when we are sufficiently humbled before him and committed to him to justify taking it on;
- greater clarity of purpose, since his vision is perfect, encompassing, and comes with his blessing;
- a compelling reason to persevere in the face of resistance and difficulty and to take risks, because you are pursuing God's directive, not merely a good idea or opportunity;
- the comfort of pursuing God's agenda rather than choosing among competing human expectations and agendas;
- the freedom to reject great opportunities by using vision as a filter, thus sparing you from being pulled in too many directions or joining forces with inappropriate partners; and
- inspiring people with hope, attracting people to a cause of value and significance, building community through the sharing of a common purpose, and sustaining people through a meaningful end.

Vision versus Mission

Sometimes people claim that they have vision when what they really have is mission. To millions of leaders the distinction is fuzzy, mere semantics, or insignificant. That view reflects ignorance of what is at stake. Accepting and understanding the distinction is vitally important; mission and vision have different purposes and impact.

Mission is the broad understanding and articulation of why you or your organization exist. It does little more than identify the industry in which you work or the primary value you serve. Mission dictates the most general parameters within which you work and helps to focus your efforts in a vague direction.

Church mission statements indicate that they exist to do ministry. Business mission statements verify their quest to make a profit and indicate the general type of work that will enable such profitability. The mission of political leaders is to help people.

What makes each of these entities successful is not their generic reason for existence but their specific sense of why God needs them in the first place—that is, their unique and distinctive calling from God to do something specific and significant. This latter perspective is the vision. Vision is the tangible development and strategic pursuit of the mission.

Mission with Vision

Possessing an understanding of your mission without a concurrent comprehension of vision raises a major problem: You will never completely accomplish the mission because it is too big, too vague, and too costly to achieve. It is the vision that moves you from the macro-perspective to the micro-perspective, narrowing your focus from the entire playing field to a specific position on it. Rather than placing you in direct and chaotic competition with everyone else, vision gives you an understanding of the unique contribution that you will make to the landscape. Mission tells you who else is interested in the same general field of activity; vision helps to give each of those players a distinct identity and direction to pursue. In other words, God's vision for you is like a fingerprint: There is no other one like it in the world.

Get comfortable with the notion that millions of people and organizations share the same mission. For instance, every Christian has essentially the same mission (to love God and love others) and every business has a similar mission (to produce value for the organization's owners and its end users by conducting some specified type of activity). It is God's carefully crafted vision for each entity that enables it to fit into his perfectly designed and interwoven fabric for the world that allows people and organizations to achieve meaning and a sense of value.

Can you succinctly articulate your vision and mission as a Christian individual? As a leader, can you state the vision and mission of the enterprise you lead?

It's Not God's Vision

Another common obstacle to transformative leadership is operating with a vision that is your vision or a group's vision but did not originate from God.

The implications are massive. Vision that we develop independent of God often conflicts with his holy and perfect plan for us. God cannot bless us or use us as if we were fully devoted to his vision, since our pursuits reflect our selfishness and spiritual immaturity.

How can you tell if a vision that moves you is from God or something of your own creation? Here are some hallmarks of God's vision:

- Human vision is based on trying to maximize our resources and skills. God's vision is based on using us beyond our capacity.
- Human vision is based on accomplishing the most appealing dream. God's vision challenges us to accomplish an impossible or improbable dream.
- Human vision is often based on what brings us delight. God's vision is a reflection of what brings him delight.
- Human vision is dangerous because it inflates our ego. God's vision is dangerous because it demonstrates his power at work within us—and our complete inadequacy.
- Human vision drives us to push ourselves to the limit. God's vision drives us to our knees in submission, humility, and obedience.
- Human vision represents a commitment we develop and pursue until we tire of the battle. God's vision becomes an obsession we embrace until he enables us to fulfill it or he brings us home.
- Human vision reflects our cultural obsessions: size, speed, status, and

success. God's vision reflects biblical obsessions: people, holiness, love, and transformation.

Goals versus Vision

We also often confuse goals and strategies with God's vision. For instance, numerous studies we have conducted show that senior pastors typically confuse teaching and numerical growth with God's vision. God's desired ends may require strong teaching and result in numerical growth, but his vision is never based on those elements.

Business leaders frequently describe their vision in terms of profit and efficiency, but those are products of vision rather than the heart of a unique calling. Political leaders frequently accept compromise and legislative outcomes as vision when those are simply by-products of the political process that may have nothing to do with vision. Ministry staffs are prone to think of vision as new programs and events, while parents often confuse control and emotional comfort with vision.

Be careful that you do not make the same mistakes. God's vision is practical but is focused on changing people to become more Christlike. This is true of every human endeavor regardless of the genre of leadership provided.

God's Vision Is Probably Not What You Expect

One of the characteristics of God's vision is that when people initially hear it, they laugh in astonishment at the bravado and utter absurdity of your seeking such an outcome. More than a few godly leaders will tell you that when they began to spread their understanding of God's vision for their group the immediate response was, *Are you kidding?*

Rest assured that God intends to show his power and his love for you by sending you on a vision journey that is way beyond your capacity. En route, you will have to rely upon him, and the results could only be attributed to God.

Let me be very clear about God's vision: It is probably not what you expect. It typically is counterintuitive because God refuses to be limited by his creation. It is not based on human consensus; his vision will stir intense emotion and debate, causing some people to seek other places through which they can serve him more comfortably while energizing others. His vision comes at a high cost because it demands significant personal change, is fulfilled only with great effort, produces results in the long term, and necessitates teams of people working together rather than individuals doing their thing in isolation. And his vision is not based on incremental improvement of others' ideas; his organizing concept for you is fresh and customized to your situation. Humankind cannot fathom the depths of God; neither can his vision be minimized by our limitations.

If you are confident you understand God's vision for your life, what has been the response of your closest friends when you shared it with them? How did the followers in the group you're called to lead react? The response you get may tell you something important about whether you are pursuing your own great ideas or God's perfect focus.

The Vision Is Not Shared

God is abundantly relational: He created us to have a relationship with him. He created us in his image, which means we are also to have significant, supportive relationships with each other. Our relational nature is linked to the reality that God's vision is too big for one person to fulfill without the help of others; that's part of the grand design.

Relationships Are Key

Effective leadership, then, demands that you develop significant, life-changing relationships with others so that you may work together to change the world for Christ, accomplishing more than you could have alone. Too often, though, the leader grasps, owns, and pursues God's vision but does not incorporate others into the process.

Your job as a leader is to assist every fellow leader and follower in adopting God's vision for the group as part of their purpose in life. To get to that stage, everyone involved must understand both the content and the context of the vision.

This requires you to articulate the vision very precisely and concisely. The language used to communicate the vision must be stirring, to the point, and memorable. You must take advantage of every opportunity to share the vision in ways that rekindle people's passion for it, commend them for their involvement, reinforce their support, and refocus their attention on it.

In most of the ministries and businesses for whom I have consulted, followers have no gripe with the vision—they simply have no sense of personal participation in its pursuit. Great leaders help individuals find their roles in pursuing the vision. It is a time-consuming task but one that is absolutely necessary if the group is to make progress toward its fulfillment.

Think about the people whom you are leading. When was the last time you sat down for a cup of coffee or lunch with each individual, one-on-one, and discussed their current understanding of the vision and their levels of commitment to and participation in it? How often do you stop the people with whom you work and compliment them for their commitment to that vision, or help them to interpret a task they had just completed in relation to the outworking of the vision?

The Vision Is on the Back Burner

Sometimes leaders get so wrapped up in the frantic pace and the multitude of tasks that must be juggled that we lose sight of the big picture and unconsciously relegate the vision to the back burner. It's not that we deem the vision irrelevant or unhelpful; we are simply so busy that we rely upon reflex actions and routines rather than using the God's vision as the primary filter through which every decision should be viewed and decided. Before you know it, we begin to compromise what we're supposed to be about and make decisions based on inappropriate factors.

Every Step You Take

The most effective leaders I have studied have so absorbed the vision that every thought, word, and action emanates from their judgment of how it intersects with whatever challenge or opportunity they are facing at the moment. These people embody the vision, and their habitual con-

> *Great leaders are the ones who first see what in retrospect, but only in retrospect, is obvious, and who have both the force of will and the authority to move people with them.*
>
> —RICHARD NIXON

sideration of it encourages others to follow suit. The vision becomes akin to a Christian mantra; leaders as well as followers become accustomed to viewing reality through a vision filter.

What was the most recent leadership decision you made? Did you run your decision through a vision filter, asking yourself if your decision maximized the opportunity to move people closer to the fulfillment of the vision? Do you habitually run your leadership decisions through a mental grid that identifies your strategic options and how each of those relates to the vision?

DISCERNING GOD'S VISION

If you do not currently understand God's vision for the group you lead, you may wonder how to go about getting that wisdom. Although it is a fairly straightforward, four-part process, I have watched people agonize over this process to no avail. Here are the insights I've gleaned from interviewing and observing godly, effective leaders.

A FISH OUT OF WATER

Know Yourself Well

Before God can use you as a leader—which is a very privileged position and thus requires people who are equipped for its challenges—you have to comprehend your strengths and weaknesses, your gifts and abilities, your emotional composure, the nature of your past successes and failures, your relational capacity, and your character flaws. This self-knowledge will give you realistic perspective—and drive you to God for strength and nurture. Portions of this journey will be painful as we come clean before God about who we really are and what truly motivates and excites us.

> *A vision without the ability to execute it is a hallucination.*
>
> —STEPHEN CASE, *AOL Time Warner*

I believe this step is critical to the Lord because it causes us to recognize our own inadequacies and to fear and trust him. Anything that deepens our intimacy with him brings him joy; when you get honest about who you are and what you can do, it should cause you to realize that you are not fit to be a leader chosen by the King. It is solely by his grace that you are permitted to lead his people anywhere.

How can you arrive at such personal insights? There are, of course, numerous tools that might help: spiritual gifts inventories, personality tests, character studies, and so forth. Conversations with trusted friends sometimes offer useful confirmation or revelations. Prayer is a crucial dimension, allowing God's Spirit to show you aspects of your nature that you may typically overlook.

Know Your Leadership Context

This includes an understanding of the heartbeat of the group you lead (and, in some cases, the organization within which it operates); an understanding of the community or environment within which the group operates; and insights into the mission, vision, and values of other leaders with whom you and your group associate.

Possessing this insight requires you to spend some time doing your homework. Talk to the people whom you wish to lead to understand what God is revealing to them. If you are leading an organization, understand its history so that you can build a bridge from its past and present to its God-ordained future. Analyze studies of the community to understand the attitudes, values, lifestyle patterns, and spiritual behaviors that prevail. Talk to other leaders involved to learn what they are about and where they are striving to take people.

Don't worry about perfection in your information gathering and analysis; this is an art, not a science. As you wade into the process, you will gain new insights and begin to realize how critical it is to possess such wisdom; God's vision never operates in a vacuum. His vision is focused on changing people, but the leader must understand what they are being changed from and the dynamics of the conditions within which they must be transformed.

Know God Intimately

Christian leaders often take the third step for granted. They assume that because they read the Bible, pray, and attend church events they have mastered this step. However, this component is not to be taken lightly. Many of the Christian leaders I have studied found that this was a very taxing and demanding, yet liberating and exhilarating element in the process. Just as a good salesperson wants to understand customers' needs in order to satisfy them, so must a Christian leader understand the mind and heart of God for the people the leader has been called to direct in order to bless God and those people.

Knowing God more completely and intimately typically involves intense Bible study and prayer. The emphasis is not simply putting in time or gathering facts but striving to truly forge a deeper and more passionate bond with the One who loves you more than we will ever comprehend. Many leaders I have interviewed revealed that they were able to take the relationship to a new level through engaging in spiritual disciplines such as fasting, meditation, and solitude.

Another aspect that many have found to be invaluable is intentionally and intently listening to the Lord as he speaks to you through whatever ways he chooses. Overall, your objectives in this relational phase are to better understand God's nature, to grasp how he provides vision to his chosen leaders, and to explore how he interacts with his leaders as they strive to implement the vision.

Test Your Conclusions

Before you start building leadership efforts around what you now think is a vision, take this final step.

First, make sure that every element of the vision is consistent with Scripture, for God neither contradicts himself nor wishes to confuse his leaders. Then get objective feedback from wise counselors—people who know you, the Lord, and your context, and who can be trusted to provide wise, honest, and confidential reactions. Finally, examine the circumstances to determine what kind of open doors or signs the Lord provides to you, if any. Taken together, these safeguards are likely to set you on the right path.

Ultimately, it seems that God takes greater pleasure in our investment in this process than he does in the eventual outcomes. He wants our hearts. After great Christian leaders give him their heartfelt love, focus, and obedience, his vision then becomes their rallying call and the object of their attention and energy.

A FEW EXAMPLES

Let's examine a few situations in which Christian leaders sought the Lord's vision for their efforts and what they learned. These examples may help you evaluate your vision more realistically.

A Christian who was CEO of a healthcare provider suggested that God's vision for the organization was *to produce healthy people, healthy relationships, and healthy profits.*

Was that God's vision? No, however laudable, that is a mission statement. It does not describe anything unique or distinctive that the organization should strive to accomplish. Every healthcare provider might adopt the same statement—a sure indicator that it is mission, not vision.

I do not know what God's vision for that facility is—only God's chosen leaders for that institution will receive that vision. (You can never tell someone else what God's vision for their life or their organization is; the best you can do is confirm that a vision statement does or does not have the marks of true vision.) However, in contrast, the vision statements of other healthcare providers are more on target:

- To provide the highest quality medical care in the region and be the premier cardiac care provider in the state;
- To improve the mental, physical, and emotional health of people in (community name) through the implementation of an aggressive preventative medicine strategy;
- To provide free or minimal-cost health care services of the highest caliber for individuals and families who lack the means to pay for such services.

Here's another example. A woman leading a small group defined her vision statement as *providing a safe place for people to discover the Word and purposes of God.* Again, as helpful as that concept is, the broad-based nature of the statement precludes it from being vision. It lacks the specificity and distinctiveness that marks God's vision. Other small-group leaders have worked hard at discerning God's visions for their groups and determined that the directions were:

- To study God's Word in depth on a weekly basis to bring about a deep and permanent healing of past traumas experienced by each group member;
- To meet regularly to examine how God calls particular believers to a ministry in global missions.

Clearly, these types of foci are not for everyone—and that is the benefit of vision: It clarifies the uncommon purpose that a particular group has in common.

Here are more some examples of how some pastors have described God's vision for their churches:

- To pursue the Great Commission and fulfill the Great Commandment;

- To exalt, evangelize, equip, and edify;
- To build a community of believers dedicated to knowing, loving, and serving Jesus Christ in all we think, say, and do.

Each is clearly a mission statement because it is a generic, broad-based depiction of what every church is called to do. Each is not detailed enough to distinguish one ministry from another, leaving all churches in an area to simply compete with each other and to provide overlapping if not identical ministry.

Sometimes churches (and other types of organizations) embrace cute statements that are neither mission nor vision. *To reach the lost at any cost*, for example, is unbiblical, since Scripture tells us to always count the cost of any endeavor, and the statement focuses solely upon one aspect in which every church is called to participate (evangelism).

To preach the gospel to the whole world is a partial mission statement—broad and ministry focused, but both incomplete and not unique, since every church is called to do this. *To build a church of 5,000 people by 2010* is one of the clearest examples of human vision, since God does not limit his vision through arbitrary dates and numbers. If anything, this is a goal statement, not a description of God's vision.

Questions to Ask

As you examine a draft vision statement there are some questions that help evaluate its authenticity:

- Does the central concept describe something that is unique to that entity?
- Is the admonition on which the statement is focused motivating and compelling?
- Is the underlying purpose that of seeing lives transformed in accordance with God's expressed purposes?
- Is the vision people-oriented?
- Does the vision provide a specific direction for the group to pursue, including the identity of a target group to influence?

- Is the proposed outcome audacious—too big to accomplish by human power and wisdom alone? Does the magnitude of the vision make you uncomfortable?
- Is it consistent with biblical principles and values?

Vision Statement Examples

Now let's look at some vision statements that seem to reflect the calling of God.[2]

- To equip professionals in Manhattan to impact their web of personal and professional relationships through cell group and marketplace ministries that lead people to the Cross and to Christian community. (Vision of a church in New York City)
- To provide my children with the skills, experiences, and resources that would enable them to return to their native country someday to make Christ known and provide his love to others in tangible ways. (Vision of parents who adopted two children from Central America)
- To produce quality products, quality relationships, and an above-average profit stream that enables the company to annually reinvest a minimum of 6 percent of its profits into community services benefiting the disadvantaged. (Vision of a manufacturing firm serving a national clientele)
- To devote my life to leading and building up congregations that will plant new churches in areas where the church is inadequately present, and to invest personal energy in identifying, training, and supporting individuals from within those congregations whom God has called to be church planters. (Vision of a pastor serving an independent church)
- To develop the talents of my coworkers to their fullest extent by identifying and funding their developmental needs, while modeling the life of Christ and a commitment to raising the moral and ethical standards of the company and our clients. (Vision of a department head in a corporation in the hospitality industry)

A Fish Out of Water

You might quibble with some of the phrasing of any given statement, but you can see how these statements would motivate believers to sense their unique purpose in their immediate environment and to devote significant personal resources toward impacting the lives of specific people.

Making the Most of the Vision

Vision is a tool that helps leaders focus themselves and those who follow them. How can you use it as God intends?[3]

Once you discern the vision, develop the habit of thanking God for his trust in you and for the challenge the vision presents. This is his gift to you—and it comes with an ironclad guarantee that leaders who devote themselves to its pursuit will be blessed.

One of the best ways to demonstrate your gratitude is to become a tireless champion of the vision. In that role you become the primary role model, spokesperson, and protector of the vision. Assist others in understanding and owning it. Relate all decisions to it, motivate involvement based on it, mobilize people around its pursuit, and use it to generate the resources necessary to fulfill the vision.

Craft a brief statement that encapsulates the core substance of the vision and encourage followers to learn and adopt that statement as part of their calling, assisting them in finding their appropriate role in its pursuit.

Reflect and Refocus

As a leader, you should intentionally devote a portion of your schedule to meditating on the vision from time to time. Reflect on the contours of the concept, what you have done recently to pursue it, what those efforts produced and taught you, and the new opportunities that are emerging in your vision quest. Refocusing addresses our tendency to get distracted and complacent. Never let your passion for the vision flame out! Understanding God's vision is a process in which he progressively reveals more of the vision as you prove your commitment. The vision comprehension process is a lifelong project that is based on your desire and God's revelation; plan now to habitually carve out time to shape that vision.

CORPORATE VERSUS PERSONAL VISION

Perhaps you have noticed that there are two different levels of vision that you may possess: personal vision and corporate vision. Every Christian should have a clear understanding of God's unique purpose for his or her life. All believers have the same mission (see Luke 10:27, for example), and yet every one of us has a unique purpose in God's greater plan for the world. It is important that you have a firm grasp of that personal vision because it will impact your leadership by helping you to know which situations are appropriate for you to take on as a leader and how to lead people most effectively.

For the sake of clarity, here's a personal example. God's vision for my life is *to be a catalyst of a moral and spiritual revolution in the United States.* That vision, birthed after hours and hours of prayer, substantial Bible study, and much effort at achieving self-awareness, has helped me to reject dozens of great opportunities during my life. It caused me, for instance, to forego some attractive opportunities in other nations, since my focus is to be the United States. It has helped me to recognize that profit is less important than opportunities to have moral and spiritual influence. It has led me to seek relationships with particular individuals and organizations with whom I would not be naturally inclined to interact, but who have become significant partners in laying a foundation for cultural transformation in America.

Toward that end, we began the Barna Research Group in the belief that information is a powerful and valuable tool that can help to shape strategic decisions. Thus the vision statement of the Barna Research Group is *to provide current, accurate, and reliable information, in bite-sized pieces, at reasonable cost, so that ministries can make more strategic decisions.*

In other words, my self-perception and personal vision from God shaped my corporate activity, initiating a company that used my skills, education, passion, and experiences to form an organization designed to help ministries act strategically in the moral and spiritual development of America. Barna Research Group is a means to the end for which I believe God created and called me.

I do not mean to draw attention to myself and certainly do not claim to have done everything to perfection—far from it. There are as many lessons to draw from the countless mistakes I've made as from the successes the Lord has allowed us to experience. There are thousands of people, companies, and ministries I have encountered who have a similar story to tell.

Is yours one of them?

If so, carry on good and faithful servant! Help other leaders to understand the process that you have undertaken in service to God. As Psalm 103:2 exhorts us, "Praise the Lord, O my soul, and forget not all his benefits."

If you have not clarified your personal vision and, as a leader of others, the vision for the group you are called to lead, commit to making the vision the centerpiece of your life and leadership efforts. Do whatever it will take to gain God's revelation. As a result of that understanding and commitment, your life and the lives of those you lead will never be the same!

Valerie's Return

You may be wondering what happened to Valerie after her eye-opening annual review and subsequent revelation about her lack of vision. Her first move was to switch her vision statement to be her ministry's mission statement. Next, she threw herself into the task of more deeply understanding the vision process. She realized that if she was missing the mark in this regard, most of the people in the church probably were as well, so vision development would be one of the compo-nents of the discipling process at the church—once she understood it!

After a couple months of tireless effort at discerning God's vision for the church's discipleship ministry, Valerie conferred with

> *Vision becomes a living force only when people truly believe they can shape their future.*
> —PETER SENGE

her three closest advisers to share her sense of the vision. After some tweaking, she met with the senior pastor to gain his reaction, which was excitement and a pledge of support. She then called together the lay leaders involved in the discipleship ministry for a special meeting—her first genuine "vision casting" session in which she revealed the vision, the process that had led to it, and a plan for how they might start to incorporate the vision in their common and individual ministries. Valerie subsequently spent several hours per week getting together with those leaders one-on-one to talk about their personal vision and how they would inte-grate their skills and gifts into the pursuit of the church's discipleship vision. She was intent upon getting people's ownership of and commitment to the vision.

Getting the congregation to embrace the vision was a different story. They were slow to come around because they had already been exposed to and focused on a different understanding of the church's discipleship process. Eventually, however, people became enamored of the concept and lives began to change in ways that could be traced back to the clarity and power of the vision. Valerie ceased to motivate people on the strength of her charm, energy, good ideas, and intriguing events. Congregants became excited about the potential outcomes because they "got it." Less energy was devoted to big programs and special events; more effort was poured into relational ministries built on studying the Bible, applying its principles, and being held accountable by fellow believers. Transformation happened first in Valerie's life through her understanding and adoption of God's vision, then in the lives of many others who were touched by that vision.

For the record, here is the vision statement that Valerie crafted for the discipleship ministry: "For young congregants to regularly work in close, long-term relationships with mature Christians—forming a *discipling unit*—to nurture a biblical worldview and to accept loving accountability for character, beliefs, and behavior by the church's elders."

Uncomfortable Questions

- If I were to interview the people involved in the group you lead and asked them to recite the vision for your shared efforts, what would I hear?
- What in the vision you have been given makes your focus unique and compelling?
- How many times today did you bring up the vision in conversation with the people you are leading?
- In what ways does each of the decisions you made today conform to the vision you are pursuing? Are there any decisions you made that conflict with that vision?
- On what basis do you motivate your followers to stay enthusiastic and involved?

—5—

We cannot find the stuff of leadership in the dry pages of a history text. To find it, we have to look into the spirit of the man to see what it is that sustains and drives him and enables him to drive or to persuade others.

—RICHARD NIXON

CHAPTER FIVE

It's What's Inside That Matters

MARY WAS A CLASSIC OVERACHIEVER. After graduating from an Ivy League college in three years she immediately pursued her MBA at a leading business program and graduated with honors. From there she landed a plum position in a top-notch management consulting firm in New York. For several years she jumped from one prestigious firm to another, clawing her way up the executive ranks. Before she hit age thirty Mary was a vice president at a major publishing company in the Big Apple.

A few years later Mary was approached by the executive committee of the corporation with an invitation to launch a new publishing company under the corporation banner. The committee chose Mary because of her impressive leadership skills. She was one of their best strategic thinkers, an excellent communicator, and had a deft touch for hiring talented employees away from competitors. She also was absolutely vigilant about profitability, consistently lit a fire under her team; and instituted procedures for ruthless in-house evaluation that led to continual internal renewal and improvements.

Mary accepted the offer with enthusiasm and did not disappoint her seniors.

A Fish Out of Water

After spending a couple of months doing her homework, she presented a strong business plan and was given the approval and funding to launch the new imprint. She hired an experienced and aggressive team of colleagues, made waves in the industry, and threw herself into the project 110 percent.

Yet, five years into the life of the company, something was clearly wrong with Mary's venture. The promising concept had never fully taken off. Although the company had devoted the necessary resources to building brand awareness and developing a unique product line, the company seemed strangely "flat" on the inside. No matter how much cheerleading and motivational energy Mary poured into the organization, great coworkers invariably departed within months, hard-won authors fulfilled their contracts then left for other publishers, and agents protected their clients from the promises and royalty advances offered by the firm.

The heart of the problem? Mary. Another large New York publishing firm, not known for shying away from controversial executives, was appalled at some of her antics. Chagrined, the executive committee fired Mary from the division she had created, one week shy of her sixth anniversary.

What finally swayed the committee? Feedback from her coworkers and sub-contractors. She was described as a corporate tiger who would do anything—lie, steal, beg, maim, cheat—to get her way. In spite of paying top dollar for industry talent, she had trouble hanging on to good employees; after all, who wanted to be known as one of "Mary's Mercenaries"? Even strong, experienced industry professionals who thought they had seen it all shied away from the opportunity to work alongside her. The ruthless practices ridiculed in many of the novels she published were the same attributes that ultimately toppled her from corporate leadership.

What Is Character?

Most likely Mary was not paying attention when her business classes were exposed to the work of Warren Bennis, the dean of leadership analysts in America. Among his profound insights is this gem:

It's What's Inside That Matters

In the leadership arena, character counts. I am not saying this casually. My convictions about character-based leadership come from years of studies, observations, and interviews with leaders and with the people near them. . . . I've never seen a person derailed from [leadership] positions for lack of technical competence. But I've seen lots of people derailed for lack of judgment and character.[1]

Character matters. The word *character* is derived from a Greek term that refers to engraving, implying that character is the sum of the indelible marks imprinted on you which shape your thoughts and behavior. Character is your inner substance— the content of your heart that is manifested through your behavior and values. Character, in other words, is who you are when nobody's looking. The real you.

Character produces visible qualities such as personality, preferences, ideology, image, values, lifestyle, and reputation; it is responsible for shaping what we think, how we act, and what we value.

Jesus' ministry was largely concerned with character. For instance, his teaching in Matthew 15 was designed to help the disciples to understand the significance of character. "Don't you see that whatever enters the mouth goes into the stomach and then out of the body?" Jesus asks. "But the things that come out of the mouth come from the heart, and these make a [person] 'unclean.' For out of the heart come evil thoughts, murder, adultery, sexual immorality, theft, false testimony, slander. These are what make [someone] 'unclean.'"[2]

> *Character is destiny.*
> —HERACLITUS

Given the apparent importance of character, then, we must wonder about the source of character. Almost by definition, good character is stable and consistent; people must be able to rely on its steadiness and rightness. To reach such a level, character must be based on a reliable and unchanging standard. That standard is the Bible. It provides people with a tangible, constant definition of right and wrong that may be used to guide our choices and development. For Christians who are leaders the Bible represents the repository of character-shaping wisdom.

It is vital that you take this matter to its logical conclusion, though, and acknowledge that as a follower of Christ, your character must be based on the standard of absolute moral truth. The alternative—moral relativism—leads to confusion, chaos, and tolerance of sin and depravity as a personal right. The people you lead deserve the best guidance you can provide, direction that is consistent, intelligent, morally appropriate, rational, and based upon proven principles. None of those needs can be satisfied through judgment based upon feelings and other subjective, transitory factors. If you want to be a Christian leader, you must know and live in concert with God's principles.

> *Successful leadership is not about being tough or soft, assertive or sensitive. It is about having a particular set of attributes which all leaders, male or female, seem to share. And chief among these attributes is character.*
>
> —WARREN BENNIS

Does this challenge make you uncomfortable? My research has shown that a majority of Christians who are leaders do not believe in absolute moral truth and do not base their moral choices on biblical principles. Is there any wonder, then, why churches are in disarray, why Christian marriages dissolve at the same rate as those of non-Christians, or why nonbelievers consider the Christian faith reasonable but Christians to be hypocrites? What kind of character undergirds your leadership?

WHY CHARACTER COUNTS

At its core, leadership is about developing a symbiotic relationship between the leader and the follower. In an ideal environment, the leader takes his cues from

God, developing morals, values, and core beliefs based upon the standards set by God. The leader then turns around and provides cues to his followers, whose morals, values, and core beliefs are shaped by the model presented by the leader. Character is, therefore, significant because it is the root of a leader's influence. What leaders say and do are a reflection of who they are at their most elementary level—the place where character resides.

Character makes or breaks a leader, because it either does or does not provide people with a compelling reason to follow. Vision gets people's attention, makes them think, and gets them excited. But unless the leader has the character to support the vision, people will remain skeptical and seek alternatives. We have all learned—often through painful experiences—that if you want to figure out where a leader is likely to take us, it is wiser to investigate his character than his public statements about future plans. No wonder Proverbs 29:2 informs us that, "When the righteous thrive, the people rejoice; when the wicked rule, the people groan."

> *Be more concerned about your character than your reputation. Your character is what you really are, while your reputation is merely what others think you are.*
> —DALE CARNEGIE

Most people have become fairly savvy consumers of leadership, and their dominant questions relate to character. A powerful example of this is the presidential campaigns of the past decade. The news media have been roundly criticized by the intelligentsia for focusing on "soft news"—in other words, character issues and personal profiles—more than on candidates' stands on the issues. News executives typically respond that voters are less interested in a person's perspectives, which may change over time, and more interested in who they are. People vote for candidates on the basis of character as much as, if not more than, any other attribute.

Gail Sheehy reports that people carefully study leaders before consenting to follow in order to protect themselves against a leader who is likely to make bad decisions on their behalf, to get more realistic insight into the nature of the leader than that provided by the public persona, and to determine whether the leader will serve as a practical model of a superior moral life.[3] In more than a quarter-century of analyzing how the public selects its political leaders, she concludes that people are instinctively driven to search the character of those who wish to lead. Yes, you can still fool some of the people some of the time, but that trick is getting harder and harder to pull off.

Countering a Fatal Attraction

For Christians, the issues surrounding whom to follow are even deeper. Because believers realize that we all have a tendency, if not a fatal attraction, to sin, placing ourselves under the authority of a godly leader becomes a significant spiritual act. When we consent to a person's leadership, we are doing more than agreeing to some type of loose association. We are inviting that individual to choose paths for us that will either protect us from, or subject us to, temptation and evil. The character of the leader is the deliberating influence that dictates which path will be chosen in any given situation.

Do you believe you have been called by God to lead people? If so, then people deserve insight into what rules your character: an earnest and intense love of God or a desire to master and please the world. It has been suggested that every Christian undergoes an internal battle between self-interest and servanthood. A leader who is truly Christian is able to transcend selfish motives through the empowerment of the Holy Spirit to provide direction for the common good. Such character reflects the indwelling and control of the Spirit, which earns him the right to lead and encourages followers to partner with the leader in pursuit of God's vision.

The absence of godly character, however, produces a leader whose selfish ambitions triumph. People without Christ at the center of their lives have little to restrain them from seeking what is best for themselves. Their character is based on a customized blend of beliefs and values that places themselves, rather than God, at the center. No doubt, you have even known some individuals who have accepted Christ as their Savior but have managed to dis-associate their alleged spiritual rebirth from the transformation of their character; they profess Christ as Lord, but their character does not reflect it. No matter how skilled or charismatic such a person might be, the possession of character that seeks personal honor and glory disqualifies him from the privilege of serving God by leading his people.

> *We keep rediscovering that credibility is the foundation of leadership. . . . People won't believe the message if they don't believe in the messenger. People don't follow your technique. They follow you—your message and your embodiment of that message.*
> —JAMES KOUZES

Further verification of the significance of character is found in our research. When we asked a national sample of adults to describe the attributes most important in an effective leader, character factors topped the list. Elements such as integrity, courage, and compassion were acknowledged as critical to being a leader whom people would want to follow. We realize that skills can be taught, professionals can be hired, but character is the essence of what you get when you hand over the reins to a leader.

CORE CHARACTER ATTRIBUTES

The Bible speaks volumes on the issue of the character of leaders. The Old Testament offers numerous narratives concerning the success and failure of leaders, showing that few failed because of incompetence; most of them failed because of weak character. The New Testament provides insight into the desirable character attributes of leaders through the parabolic teachings of Jesus, his modeling of appropriate character in a leader, and the writings of Paul to the leaders whom he was mentoring.[4]

Recent studies of leadership character have produced a greater awareness of how the process works. Michael Josephson writes that great leaders have character that is organized around good principles (the things they believe), a sensitive conscience (an internalized sense of right and wrong), and moral courage (the internal strength to do what is right).[5] A person with such a combination of attributes invariably makes appropriate choices and helps others to move in an appropriate direction.

What are the character traits of people whose leadership exudes a truly Christian nature? The Bible goes to great lengths to spell these out for us. In analyzing those attributes, it appears that we could identify them as the "Top 40" of Christ's day—forty bits of personal identity that combine to produce the new creation with a transformed mind that Paul tirelessly promoted as the mark of a Christian. To make it easier to absorb the nature of these forty traits, they can be divided into five categories: spiritual maturity, relationships, family life, integrity, and demeanor. The table on the facing page portrays those characteristics crucial to authentic Christian leadership.

Spiritual Maturity

The character of leaders who are Christians is the primary product of their spiri-tual journey. God is relentlessly refining character to the extent that we allow him to do so. As a Christian leader your character is rooted in your relationship with and devotion to God.

The Bible indicates that if you are among his chosen leaders, you must be deeply devoted to knowing, loving, and serving him. You are to be single-minded in your belief and trust in God alone. There is no room for insincere motives; a Christian leader is to have a genuine passion for being Christlike and for pleasing God.

Your determination to know, understand, and apply scriptural principles in their purest form facilitates an ever-deepening peace with God. That determination

It's What's Inside That Matters

THE CHARACTER TRAITS OF A CHRISTIAN LEADER

SPIRITUAL MATURITY	RELATIONSHIPS	FAMILY LIFE	INTEGRITY	DEMEANOR
Devout, single-minded focus on God	Eager to serve others	Loyal to spouse	Truthful and honest	Dignified
Sincere and genuine commitment	Willing to share	A parent or role model to honorable children	Trustworthy	Self-controlled
In pursuit of doctrinal purity	Forgiving of wrongs committed	Wise manager of family finances	Respectable and reputable	Disciplined
At peace with God	Loyal	Involved in an emotionally stable family	Exemplary	Responsible
Continually growing in spiritual maturity	Hospitable and welcoming	In a family that serves Christ		Humble
Relatively mature faith	Devoted to peace and understanding			Patient
Alert to evil	Fair and just			Upbeat: joyful and hopeful
Committed to the pursuit of holiness	Controlled of speech: no malice or gossip			Gentle
	Polite and respectful			Others-centered
	Attentive			Compassionate
	Accountable			
	Kind and considerate			
	Accepting of others without jealousy			

will raise a consciousness of evil and a commitment to choose and pursue holiness as the sole viable alternative to the temptations of the world.

Christians who wish to lead must be both mature and growing in their faith. Believers whose faith is immature cannot be entrusted with the care of God's people, and those who cease to grow in their knowledge and relationship with God are insufficiently committed to him to receive his trust and anointing. When people choose a leader, they must evaluate the outward manifestations of a person's heart; God alone knows what's in the heart and uses those individuals whose heart is devoted to him.

What is your character rooted in? To be qualified and empowered by God, your leadership must be an outpouring of the faith that drives your mind and heart. Are you so in love with God that your life is an authentic expression of his ways and purposes?

Relationships

Leadership revolves around the complex network of relationships between God, his leaders, and those who follow his leaders. The character of leaders is both developed by and reflected in the personal relationships they foster.

Healthy relationships are described in the Bible as those in which you look for opportunities to serve and bless other people. We are exhorted to be hospitable and welcoming toward others, attributes that enable us to build new relational bridges. The world associates leadership with being tough; in contrast, the Bible emphasizes being kind and considerate. When you lead, the focus is not you but those who follow and the One who called you to lead. Consequently, a softness of spirit is instrumental in being the type of leader who reflects the nature of God.

As a steward of God's possessions for the purpose of blessing others, you must be willing to generously share what you possess for the benefit of others and to rejoice in the success of others. There is no room for pettiness or jealousy.

This attitude is facilitated by attentiveness to people's needs and a genuine desire to build them up—even when it comes at your own expense.

> *Great minds discuss ideas. Average minds discuss events. Small minds discuss people.*
> —ADMIRAL HYMAN RICKOVER

In the course of interacting with people, there will be numerous occasions for misunderstanding and hurt. Character is formed through our enduring of and response to those hardships; godly character is proven through a Christlike response to relational difficulties. Godly character is founded on fairness and a deep passion for justice; these perspectives, in turn, promote forgiveness and loyalty.

As a leader who follows Christ, you must be committed to the relationships God has injected into your life and to strengthen them by seeking peace and understanding. How you speak to and about your friends and associates makes a difference. Godly character is reflected in the ability to control your speech, eliminating all malice or gossip. A leader who is Christian responds with civility; being polite and respectful of others, regardless of their demeanor, is always the appropriate tactic.

Scripture also encourages you to pursue relationships that will provide you with accountability. None of us is strong enough to constantly resist temptation; we gain strength from those who love us in developing sin resistance. Surrounding yourself with counselors who are wise and faithful is one of the great benefits of relationships—and one of the hallmarks of Christian leaders who remain faithful to God, true to his calling, and trustworthy to those who follow.

Who are the friends with whom you have such relationships? Are they growing in number? Do you gain discernible support through those ties? Are they helping to shape your character to be more Christlike? Are you enabling them to develop a more godly character?

A Fish Out of Water

Among the most important relationships in leaders' lives are those with their families. It is through family ties that your character becomes most transparent and irrefutable.

If you are married, how you treat your spouse is important. Do you honor your mate? Are you loyal? If you have children, who they become is another window into your true character. Are your children obedient and respectful? Is your family devoted to Christ? Grandparents, aunts, uncles, in-laws—family members of all types—influence their kinfolk, and the nature of that effect must be taken seriously.

As Paul wrote regarding those who seek to lead within the church, "If anyone does not know how to manage his own family, how can he take care of God's church?"[6] The issue is intriguing. People have questioned the relationship between a person's family and his or her qualifications as a Christian leader. It seems that it is a matter of priorities. As a Christian, your primary purpose is always to know, love, and serve God with all that you have. As a leader, your purpose is to direct people to make the right choices. As a Christian leader, then, your ultimate purpose is to serve God by leading people to appropriate decisions—and the most important decision anyone will ever make is to wholeheartedly follow Christ. The people with whom you will have the greatest influence are those who know you best—your family. If your spouse and offspring choose a different path, this speaks volumes about your ability to direct people, through whatever means necessary or appropriate, to do what is right. Often, their rejection of Christ is more a statement about your true character and spiritual commitment as a representative of Christ than it is a genuine repudiation of the Savior.

The Bible goes on to suggest that how you manage your family's resources is another clue as to your character. This includes money as well as time, possessions, relationships, ideas, and other treasures. The way you handle your resources relates to your character because it reveals the things that are important to you and, through that revelation, your potential as a Christian in leadership.

What will others learn about your character by observing your family? Have you invested sufficient time and energy in their lives? Do they respond to your leadership?

Integrity

Leaders who have integrity demonstrate what it means to be in the image of God. Integrity implies being truthful and honest, enabling people to rely on your word and motives. People of integrity are trustworthy, which fosters confidence in the leader's decisions and behavior. Truth and trust are foundations on which a relationship with a leader are built; the absence of these qualities breeds insecurity, doubt, and independence—all of which undermine the unity, strength, and dependability that is a leader's responsibility.

A person of integrity is also worthy of respect because he or she is a known commodity and reputable. In fact, a key to godly character is being exemplary—a role model whom others can imitate with the confidence that they are learning appropriate behaviors.

> *Integrity is like oxygen; the higher you go, the less there is of it.*
> —PAUL DICKSON

Integrity produces credibility; credibility facilitates the right to lead. As the people you lead assess your character, what degree of credibility do they assign to you? How many of them want to be like you—even if they do not want the headaches and pressures that come with leadership?

Demeanor

The way that you, as a leader, think of yourself significantly affects how people respond to you. Do they sense humility—the comprehension that apart from God you can do nothing of value and have no meaningful direction to give? Do they sense an upbeat spirit, based upon your joy in knowing Christ and your unshakable hope in the future because of his enduring love? Do they experience patience with those who need guidance, emanating from the recognition that leadership is a high calling that demands hard work?

The character of mature leaders who are Christian stems from a love that is gentle and others-centered. Leaders make tough decisions and must demonstrate backbone in the midst of tension and conflict. Yet, their character bleeds through those situations to show compassion and caring. Leaders who are called by God to lead are simply being obedient; they are born to lead, yet the motivation for leading is a desire to please God by caring for his people. That attitude gives them a certain dignity in who they are and how they lead.

Effective leadership requires a disciplined mind and heart—not only in response to opportunities to sin but also in relation to practical decision-making, the development of community among followers, and the assessment of opportunities. Because they understand their human limitations and recognize the magnitude of their calling, great leaders who are Christian are responsible and self-controlled.

What you do and how you do it matters. As your followers observe you from day to day, what behavioral traits do they admire in you?

A CHARACTER SMORGASBORD?

Keep in mind that even though our discussion involves a long list of attributes, Christians who want to be qualified to lead are called to embody all of these elements, not merely a customized selection of them. Leadership is a high calling and not one to be taken for granted. When God calls a leader, he sets the bar high, very high, but he also enables that individual to clear the bar in due course.

However, before you surrender to the feeling that the standard is beyond your reach, recognize that none of us can completely reflect all of these wonderful and attractive attributes. God does not expect you to be perfect. His desire is for you to embrace these character outcomes as your goal and to arduously work toward incorporating them into your character.

Perhaps the biblical King David is a reasonable role model. Here was a talented and blessed leader who loved God and yet was guilty of adultery and murder, among other sins. Not even those unseemly behaviors permanently disqualified him from leadership, though, because the desire of his heart was to love and honor God. What is the bottom-line desire of your heart?

> *A leader with drive but not competence and integrity is a demagogue. One with competence but not integrity is a technocrat. One with ambition and competence but not integrity is a destructive achiever.*
>
> —WARREN BENNIS

DEVELOPING SOLID CHARACTER

During the past several years I have been intrigued to find that there is a hierarchy of expectations related to character. Americans have the highest expectations regarding the character of leaders, whether they lead in a business, government, or religious context. They have somewhat lower expectations of the character of the people with whom they have contact. They have the lowest standards for their own character.

Therefore, apart from what this implies personally and to those who help to shape people's character and expectations, this means that leaders get tougher scrutiny and must live up to a higher standard. Is that fair? Absolutely! Leaders ought to be held to higher standards. They have influence on people's lives. Leadership is a spiritual act of worship and guidance. Wouldn't you want people to take their moral and spiritual cues from individuals who reflect the best character possible?

For those of us in leadership this raises the question of how to continually enhance our character. Really, this is the basic question of discipleship: How can we constantly become more Christlike?

No Secrets to Spiritual Development

I won't attempt to provide you with a handful of tidy little secrets to the spiritual life you always wanted. Real discipleship requires more than a handful of habitual practices, and your spiritual development will never be tidy. Besides, there are no secrets regarding spiritual growth since the Bible lays out the necessary principles for us. Nevertheless, there are some thoughts to consider.

Your character is like a muscle—it must be regularly exercised to become stronger. If you wish to be a person of good character, you must adopt appropriate habits, practices that produce desired outcomes. In order to identify the habits worth integrating into your life, you must first figure out the nature of the character you hope to build. If, for instance, you accept the "Top 40" attributes described above, then you may wish to evaluate where you currently stand in relation to each of those and then devote yourself to improving in areas of weakness.[7]

Fashioning a Spiritual Regimen

If you have examined your character and feel disappointed at what you have discovered, don't get down on yourself. Good character must be learned; it does not happen automatically. After all, you and I are beset by a sinful nature. It takes a conscious and strategic effort along with a willingness to allow the Holy Spirit to do a supernatural turnaround within us before we are likely to see much progress.

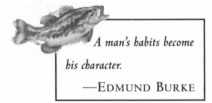

A man's habits become his character.
—EDMUND BURKE

To draw you closer to God and facilitate the development of strong character, fashion a spiritual regimen that builds on the character foundation that's already in place. Each of us needs to focus our energy in different degrees on different dimensions, but here are the core elements in helping you to make progress toward leading with the character that God wants you to possess.

It's What's Inside That Matters

Regular Study of the Bible

God defines character in the Bible and gives us all that we need to pursue it: the principles, role models, descriptions of consequences, and encouragement. Craft a plan for how you will discover compelling insights from his Word into the character elements that need buffing up in your life, whether that is doing a word study, exegeting specific passages related to the trait of interest, or scrutinizing the life of a biblical leader who wrestled with the same challenge. You should always be involved in some type of intentional and focused study that is building up your leadership capacity.

Frequent Worship and Prayer

If your character is supposed to reflect God's character, you certainly want to know him more closely. God reveals himself to you through worship and prayer, as well as his written Word. Spend time interacting with the living God and allowing him to shape and mold you through your ever-intensifying relationship with him. Bring your needs and concerns regarding your character before him in prayer. He *wants* to help you reflect him more perfectly.

Qualified, Bible-Based Instruction

You will never learn too much or know enough of the Bible. But sometimes we get glassy-eyed from going over the same portions of Scripture again and again. An objective, trained teacher of the Bible can push you to depths you did not know existed. These days we have so many great teachers available on a 24/7 basis, thanks to the Internet. If you can't get what you need from the teachers at your church, you have no excuse: Christian radio, Christian books, special teaching events, and distance education options supplement the wealth of content accessible through the Internet.

Accountability for Specific Outcomes

Left to our own devices, we often push ourselves in areas of great personal concern but let other areas slide. The way around complacency regarding character development is to place yourself under the authority of trusted, mature believers who vow to hold you accountable for specific growth. Such a process only works if you voluntarily submit and remain committed to it. The encouragement and pressure of such a process can help you get to the next level.

Experience and Reflection

Character is never developed in a vacuum. Ascertain what you wish to develop and then work at it. At the end of each day, spend a few minutes reflecting on your experiences and how your character was embodied in each of those reactions. Some leaders have said that keeping a journal of these reflections is a valuable learning tool, enabling them to review past lessons and to recognize progress. No matter which approach works best for you, be sure to test your character through the crucible of daily encounters. Character is not a theoretical construct; it is the incarnation of your spirit.

Who Are You?

Perhaps you are like Mary, the fired publisher, assuming that competencies are the lifeblood of leadership. I know I shared that belief for years. It wasn't until I began to study effective leaders who were Christians that the significance of character became apparent.

Naturally, not every leader who has great skills and mediocre character gets canned, like Mary did; many of them lead corporations and government agencies throughout the nation. But that's not your concern, nor mine. Those individuals must answer to their boards or ownership for their practices. You and

I answer to God, and he has made it clear that the requirements for leadership include righteous character.

When all the talk about character is done, it's time to deliver—and you can't deliver what you don't possess. If your character isn't up to snuff, then commit yourself to changing who you are.

Some people protest that this is a foolish desire because people cannot change. What do you think: Can Christians called to leadership by God change their character? If you have doubts, you lack faith and knowledge. Read the stories of Moses the murderer, David the adulterer, Paul the persecutor of Christians, or Peter the frightened fisherman. Once they turned to God and devoted themselves to becoming the people he wanted them to be, they were able not only to upgrade their character by the power of God but to lead so remarkably well that we still study their behavior more than two millennia later.

> *The effective leaders I have met, worked with, and observed behaved in much the same way. . . . They made sure that the person they saw in the mirror in the morning was the kind of person they wanted to be, respect, and believe in. They fortified themselves against the leader's greatest temptations—to do things that are popular rather than right, and to do petty, mean, sleazy things.*
>
> —PETER DRUCKER

With the Holy Spirit's Help

If you are willing to grow and are committed to change, it will happen—not overnight and not without pain and effort, but through the reconstructive work of the Holy Spirit, your character can be enhanced.

Always remember that who you are speaks much louder than the words you utter. If you want people to follow you, let them know who you are—not by statements and plans and position papers but through your character. Let them see your heart in action, let them understand how your mind works, invite them to join you on a journey of the imitation of Christ. Help them to understand that a Christian who leads can generate record profits for her corporation—and that it can be accomplished without cutting corners or stabbing people in the back. Enable them to realize that coaching a ball team requires sharp leadership skills, but that winning at the expense of their principles is not a win at all. Teach those who watch you how important it is to base judgment calls on what is right rather than what is expedient or expected.

In the end, a Christian cannot effectively lead without character any more than a sinner is able to enter heaven without Christ. Are you ready to let your character attract people to the cause you promote? Are you ready to let them see who you really are?

Uncomfortable Questions

- If your children, nieces, nephews, or godchildren had the same character that you currently possess, how satisfied would you be? What character traits would you encourage them to improve?
- Who are the accountability partners you rely upon to keep your character in line? How close do you let them get to the *real* you?
- What criteria do you use to evaluate the quality of your character?
- How convinced are you that the Bible provides absolute moral truths that serve as the basis for determining and developing your character?

—6—

> *Great leadership is not a zero-sum game. What is given to the leader is not taken from the follower. Both get by giving.*
>
> —GARRY WILLS

CHAPTER SIX

If You Want Good Followers, Create Them

OR THE SIXTH TIME in the past eight years, Scott had accepted a position to manage a congressional campaign. He was convinced that directing election campaigns was one of the most difficult jobs in America, but once politics gets in your blood, it's nearly impossible to resist its lure. So here he was again, managing the campaign of a first-time candidate, a businessman with deep pockets and enough self-confidence to make Bill Clinton look shy. Scott wasn't sure this candidate had much to say, but after four straight victories—two of them with candidates for whom the label dark horse would have been an exaggeration—Scott felt pretty good about his chances in this race.

Scott was the third manager in six months to take the helm of the campaign, though. His predecessors had been dismissed without remorse by the candidate. "They were nice guys," he explained to Scott when they first met to discuss the job, "but nice guys finish last. When you sign on with me, you sign on to play tough, play hard, and most of all, you sign on to win. That's our bottom line."

The campaign was a mess. It was hemorrhaging money, blowing important publicity opportunities, and losing ground in the polls. What little internal structure that existed was in jeopardy of collapsing at any moment, and Scott wasn't sure that would be disadvantageous. His challenge was to institute order, efficiency, unity, and momentum. He knew he had his work cut out for him big time.

After sizing up his resources, Scott was dismayed. The staff was average, at best, and most of them were *untouchable*—children of major donors, cousins of party officials, spouses of influential officeholders, and so forth. They had not landed these jobs by possessing useful skills or outworking the competition. The volunteers were no better. They generally showed up at a campaign office, took up space, and left with little to show for their presence. They were after a little fun, being around power, making some valuable contacts—oh, and if the candidate got elected, that'd be swell, too.

Scott created a viable strategic plan to get the campaign on track. He met with the candidate and his closest advisers—the money men—and laid out the plan. The candidate was pleased with the strategy and encouraged Scott to get rolling. The young manager took his cue and went for the throat. "But I need your support on the personnel side," he stated forcefully, looking the candidate directly in the eye. "We'll never get this campaign off the ground with the sad sack of staff we've got on the payroll. And the volunteers are just as bad. You need to give me something to work with."

The candidate broke eye contact and looked in his lap for a moment. He sighed, then looked up again, piercing Scott with a cold stare. "Listen to me, Scott, and listen good. I hired you to manage this campaign. Nothing in this world is ideal, least of all politics." He stood, leaned over the table between them and put his face inches from Scott's. "You want better people? I'm sorry, Harvard's faculty was previously engaged. So work with what you've got. I've provided the bodies and the resources to keep them onboard. It's your job to whip them into shape."

Scott was taken aback. He didn't have time to draw a breath before the candidate thundered on.

"Do you really think that I made my money in business by sitting back while world-class professionals just happened to waltz in the door looking for something to do with their time? No way, buddy, I had to mold them into a tough-as-nails army that lived to cover my rear while I breathed life into their future.

"When you took this job you told me you have strong leadership skills. Well, let's see 'em. This is what leaders do, Scott: We transform peons into partners, so we can make a dream come true."

The candidate stood up straight, without shifting his glare from Scott's face. "And Scott, if you can't do it, I'll get someone who can. Now grow me some competent followers."

NURTURING EFFECTIVE FOLLOWERS

Scott's big-headed candidate may have been demeaning, but he got one thing right: Leaders must shape their followers.

Recall that we've said that leadership is the art of helping people to grow by enabling them to embrace God's vision and pursue it with energy and passion. Such progress requires more than talk; it demands purposeful action by both the leader and his or her followers. Even when a leader is more concerned about personal power than the purposes of God and the best interests of others, he still might point followers in the right direction. If they're able to concentrate on God's vision and play a significant part in its pursuit, then it becomes a win-win situation.

And just as leaders need education and training to achieve their maximum impact, so do followers need assistance in living up to their potential. Leaders cannot bring God's vision to fulfillment on their own. They gain ground only through partnership with a supporting cast. Investing in that "cast" is one of the critical functions of a leader.

The failure to make that investment leaves the leader with role players incapable of delivering results. Remember, the enduring legacy of leaders is not the buildings they construct, the profits they earn, or the recognition they generate for their brands. It's the quality of the people they mentor and how God is able to use them for greater things than would have been possible without a unified effort.

When all is said and done, the mark of great leaders is that they empowered others to live positive and meaningful lives. To accomplish that end, leaders do not do something *to* people but do something *with* them.

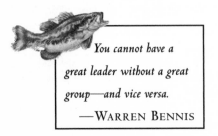

You cannot have a great leader without a great group—and vice versa.
—WARREN BENNIS

In my wide wanderings I've found that coaches of athletic teams are among the leaders most likely to understand the importance of intentionally developing the skills and character of their followers. Coaches schedule practices to raise the players' skill levels. They work one-on-one with selected players to overcome their individual weaknesses. They emphasize fulfillment and excellence to develop camaraderie and team spirit. They give pep talks to their players to keep them encouraged and focused. And they go over recent performances to celebrate successes and identify ways to improve.

That is a huge investment in their players—and all that simply to play games! Why would we assume that athletes need mentoring, but not the volunteers who serve at church or a charitable organization, the employees who work with us on the job, and even our children and spouse?

We so far have mentioned many things that make a leader great. We've said great leaders have a total devotion to a unique vision from God. They demonstrate the moral courage to direct people appropriately. They genuinely love and care about people. They have enviable character. And they possess an unquenchable thirst for learning.

Now, consider all of those leadership qualities—and then realize that they are crucial to attracting, creating, and nurturing a group of followers who work together to achieve significant common goals. The related skills then raise people's sights beyond anything they might have imagined or been able to accomplish without your guidance. But they need you to help them get there.

Do you want to raise the level of your team? As the leader you must help your followers to grow. The way to do that is by investing in three core components:

> *The leader's first job is to be a missionary, to remind people what is special about them and their institutions.*
> —CHARLES HANDY

- the *culture* of your organization,
- the *cause* to which you want them to commit, and
- the *capacity* you wish them to fulfill.

BUILDING A SOLID CULTURE

Culture may be one of those terms that gets thrown around a lot but has little tangible meaning to you. Everything contributes to your organization's culture. It can be defined as the complex intermingling of knowledge, beliefs, values, assumptions, symbols, traditions, habits, relationships, rewards, language, morals, rules, and laws that provide meaning and identity to a group of people.

A Big Blue Example

IBM sustained its success over several decades largely because of its internal culture. Its dress code, development of work teams, insistence on being the industry leader, emphasis on product excellence, giving of generous financial rewards to stalwart performers, and conservative advertising and promotional activity are factors that cannot be separated from the heart and soul of the company. People who go to work for IBM know what they are getting themselves into because they are sufficiently exposed to the company's culture prior to accepting a position. Likewise, clients know that when they deal with Big Blue there are certain things they can count on simply because they are ingrained elements of the IBM culture, regardless of who their account representative is or what type of IBM equipment they utilize.

Willow Creek Community Church has become one of a handful of model churches known throughout the nation primarily because of its internal culture. Willow Creek reinforces its unique vision by continually reiterating and modeling its corporate values. It breaks people out of the "predictable church" mold by relying on its own language (for example, *seekers, prevailing church, fully devoted followers of Christ*). Those who attend the church appreciate the regular public acknowledgment of congregants who live the church's values. Perhaps more than anything else, people who attend Willow Creek are seduced by the compelling culture of that community of faith.

Every group has a definable culture, no matter how big or small, how structured or unstructured it may be. That culture, or operating philosophy and environment, is an outgrowth of the direction and experience provided by the leader. The culture may either inspire or impair people. If your aim is to coax the maximum performance from your followers as you work toward a common goal, you must be aware of the impact of the internal culture on your people. It is a leader's responsibility to shape the culture to produce an environment that facilitates specified outcomes.

In fact, there is a continuum regarding culture development, ranging from those environments that are scrupulously shaped all the way to what might be deemed culture by default. Naturally, as a corporate culture develops, it creates a style and character that dictates the way that people within the organization think and act. It determines how the group will interpret and influence reality.

The Shape of the Future

The end result is that your group's culture shapes your future in very direct ways. The outcomes are generally predictable and connected, but there is no guarantee that your culture is healthy or productive. It becomes healthy and productive only through intentional and strategic guidance—that is, through good leadership. Such leadership interprets and responds to each situation in ways that provide meaning and purpose. Good leaders develop an empowering culture.

What does it take to develop such a positive environment for people to grow and serve within? Here are some of the commitments that healthy cultures seem to be built upon.

Leadership as Change Agent

Because a group's culture is developed in accordance with its leader's direction, you must see yourself as a change agent. This self-view sets the stage for you to think creatively, take risks, challenge people, and introduce continual renewal into the organization. By defining yourself as the person responsible for shaking things up, the culture cannot become stale and stuck in unhealthy routines unless you let it. You set the tone for the organization.

Take some time to study other organizations to figure out what style or tone fits you and your people best. In doing so you will discover that the old style of leadership in which the leader controls everything and calls all the shots (the command-and-control style) rarely works. That approach functioned well within the national culture of the forties and fifties. These days, people respond best to empowering leaders—those who want everyone to get involved and contribute something of value.

However, don't force a style or personality

> *A financial analyst once asked me if I was afraid of losing control of our organization. I told him I've never had control and I never wanted it. If you create an environment where people truly participate, you don't need control. They know what needs to be done and then do it.*
>
> —HERB KELLEHER,
> *Southwest Airlines*

upon your group, and don't try to be someone you're not. Find the right *voice*—your voice—and run with it. You're not leading IBM or Willow Creek, so don't bother to mimic their culture. (You can learn some lessons from their processes and outcomes, but you cannot be an effective clone.)

Southwest Airlines discovered the importance of uniqueness early on. Realizing they were not (and didn't want to be) United, Delta, or American, they created a very different internal culture based on hiring for attitude and training for skills. That "backward" philosophy conceived a famously distinctive culture that has served the airline well. In fact, when the rest of the industry was in the red after September 11, Southwest was still able to turn a profit.

Nurture the culture by building a spirit in which everyone is out to facilitate the best from everyone else. Champion the vision; reinforce personal commitment; develop alignment between your mission, vision, and values; and elicit meaningful participation. Your goal is to get your followers to grow by using their gifts, their judgment, and their passion toward a common end. Replace the internal competition with a drive to cooperate in pursuing the vision. Use the culture to define meaning and value. Balance the courage and toughness to make challenging decisions with a compassion for your people and purposeful relationships that transcend profits and power. Reward people for their commitment to the cause and its supporters.

Build the environment that you would want to work within if you were not in charge. Then remember: You are in charge; you can create the environment you desire.

Drawing Out the Best in People

Everyone wants to succeed, but success requires certain conditions to facilitate consistently positive outcomes. Ideally, the culture you develop will draw out the best in your people.

A major issue is for people to be emotionally involved in your joint efforts.

If You Want Good Followers, Create Them

There is nothing more debilitating than an organization in which people are simply going through the motions. Do you want to work with a group of robots? Of course not! To prevent matters from deteriorating to that point, stimulate and motivate your people to care about what they are doing. Reward them for superior performance. Celebrate progress and success. Let them have first-hand exposure to positive feedback from the people whose lives have been changed by their efforts. Continually remind them of the vision. Encourage them individually by pointing out the particulars of their personal growth. Be transparent enough to let them see and feel your passion for the cause. Whatever it takes, help them to *connect* with people and with God's special hope for your group.

Your job is to set them up for success every day. Most people are mediocre followers either because they do not know the expectations or they have not been equipped to meet them—or both. Self-assessment is an element of healthy cultures—not simply for the sake of self-awareness but to foster self-improvement. Identify the tools and resources your people will need to excel and provide them. Your people must understand that you want them to succeed, and you will do whatever it takes to help them succeed.

Failure and Accountability

There are two important components in that process. One is to tolerate temporary failure. One of the ways people learn is by trying and failing. The way that people excel is by trying, failing, learning, trying again, and succeeding. Americans have traditionally been frightened by failure at any level. That, in itself, has caused many failures. Be a big enough leader not to be threatened by temporary setbacks; see such losses as future gains. The culture you want to create is one of active learning, where risk is a part of the training regimen.

The other important factor is accountability. Not only do healthy cultures have clear and firm standards, beliefs, and convictions, they cling to those parameters in the belief that a group that stands for nothing accomplishes nothing of lasting value. Encourage appropriate interaction that leads toward personal growth and corporate productivity. This includes private, healthy-spirited constructive criticism; tough measurement standards regularly applied and fairly enforced, honest feedback; continual encouragement to grow; and the joyous celebration of others' gains. A culture that ignores or shies away from accountability invites its own demise.

Can you sense the importance of developing the right atmosphere for facilitating the kind of personal growth and world transformation that God's vision calls you to pursue? But having a nurturing environment is not enough. Beyond an affirming and empowering culture you need to provide your followers with a compelling cause.

FIXATING ON THE CAUSE

As the leader, you will not accomplish anything significant if your followers give you a halfhearted effort. Your success depends upon getting people fully committed to your cause by making it their cause as well. What is that compelling cause? It's the vision that God has called you, as a leader, to identify and pursue.

Don't make the mistake of trying to get people to fixate on you because you are the leader. Your responsibility is to get them to fixate on the vision. They must understand that they are striving for something that is bigger and more significant than one person's good idea; they are focusing on a concept that will change the world by transforming people's lives.

Ultimately, you want your people to adopt that vision as their own. It should be a source of personal identity and pride. The more intimately they embrace that purpose, the more likely they are to feel the sense of belonging that helps them forget the analytical distinctions such as leader and follower and instead focus on the desired future outcomes as a means of personal development and world impact. The more deeply they relate to those outcomes, the more they will accept the need for and process of change, the more they will push themselves beyond their assumed limits, and the more they will pursue the vision simply because it is the right thing to do.

Being a Vision Chaser

Model the life of a vision chaser. Describe how every decision you made was based on your consideration of its relation to the vision. Demonstrate your comprehension of the scope and potential influence of the vision by incorporating others into your vision quest. Let your passion for the ultimate outcomes promoted by the vision seep through as they observe you. Give evidence of the creative impulses that the vision has released within you. Lead them by example, by passion, and by the hope that the vision instills within you.

When you develop a culture that enables people to grow and focus on the pursuit of a God-given vision that is exciting, rewarding, and right, you will have their attention. But the final step toward nurturing great followers is to clarify where they fit into the picture.

CLARIFYING THEIR CAPACITY

No matter how appealing the environment and how scintillating the vision, people will withhold their complete involvement until you clarify their role in the process. Americans are among the most practical people on earth. A great vision will remain just somebody else's idea until you show people how they fit into the big picture of what you're trying to produce. If the suggested role makes sense to them, they'll get involved to the degree that their role seems to be a good fit in a productive capacity.

Once again, developing followers requires you to check your mind-set. I said you have to see yourself as a change agent. Add to that re-engineering of your role the need to be a mentor or coach to your followers. Asking people to become

A Fish Out of Water

> *Mentoring someone is not creating them in your own image, but giving them the opportunity to create themselves.*
>
> —STEVEN SPIELBERG

high-capacity role players takes more than simply communicating the vision, generating enthusiasm and buy-in, then giving them homework assignments. It will require your time to personally help them rise to the next level.

The ultimate outcomes you want to facilitate are for all followers to understand the overriding process in general, and their role in detail; to enable all followers to create value through their efforts; to grow intellectually, emotionally, and spiritually; and to experience joy and fulfillment through their involvement in the process. Doesn't that sound like the work of a coach? Really, it's simply a different way of stating the definition of what a leader does: *motivate, mobilize, resource, and direct people to pursue God's vision.*

Does this sound like hard work? It will be if you take the job seriously and do it well. Frankly, this is one of the major reasons that we have so few effective leaders today: We're so busy doing tasks that we do not sufficiently invest in growing effective followers.

Creating plans and strategies is always easier than building up people, but unless you develop people those plans and strategies are worthless. Without capable people following a focused leader, nothing of significance gets done.

What Does It Take?

A leader is an effective mentor when he helps followers to realize their personal potential and to apply their gifts and abilities to reach that potential within the framework of the vision promoted by the leader. Leaders who strive to clone themselves are not creating effective followers; those individuals will be small and shallow. To mentor a follower, the leader must heavily invest himself in the

personal growth of the follower, devoting sufficient time, energy, emotion,
prayer, and interest to enable a competent follower to emerge.

Our research regarding mentoring
has shown that the coach often grows

> *Leaders show respect for people by giving them time.*
> —MIKE KRZYZEWSKI,
> *Duke University*

during the mentoring process as much as the trainee does. Among the lessons
you must be prepared to absorb are the importance of flexing to accommodate
the different learning styles of individuals and the necessity of *aggressive listening,*
in which you listen very carefully to the feedback you get and relate it to the outcomes you are striving to inculcate. You also must remember that your goal is to
facilitate growth rather than develop a friendship, and to increasingly allow the
protégé to drive the developmental process. Invariably, one or more of these
approaches is counter to your inclination, yet we found that effective mentors
employ these methods with great effect.

Let's assume that you are ready and willing to invest the required time and
effort into building effective followers. What will it take for them to climb
onboard full force? What do they need to be effective role players?

Let me suggest that you shape their experience along five dimensions: relationships, productivity, significance, continuity, and spirituality.

Relationships

Teams that lack teamwork implode. Your job is to build an integrated group of
role players who understand their respective roles and are fulfilled in carrying
them out. Such role comprehension will include insight into those they will
interact with and the nature of those relationships. Followers should also grasp
the amount of time expected of them and to whom they are accountable in order
to build a strong network of purposeful interactions.

Some leaders resist devoting this much time and energy into helping followers see the larger picture of what they're doing and how it fits into the ultimate process. Realize that such an investment pays dividends—and the failure to make such an investment backfires. People need to understand the relational fabric and flow of your group's activity because that gives them emotional security. Without that sense of parameters and the safety it delivers, many people will derail the group's efforts due to the fear of vulnerability, confusion regarding lines of interaction, and simple mistrust.

Walking people through the relational web of your group and the importance of those interactions will come more naturally to some leaders than to others. For instance, this process is often seen as a waste of valuable time to strategic leaders, while it can be overemphasized by team-building leaders. Take a balanced perspective into this arena: You merely try to set up your followers for success based upon a viable understanding of their role in a larger course of action and the interaction they must have with others to allow the entire organization to move forward.

Productivity

Have you ever had people whom you thought were in the flow of the group's activity only to discover later that they failed to produce anything of value because they really did not understand their role? It's a common problem: Leaders, being independent and aggressive, assume that an inspiring vision talk and a clear strategic plan will necessarily lead to productive energy from followers. Keep in mind that leaders think and act differently from most of their followers; every assumption you make is a minefield waiting to explode.

Earlier in the book I noted that leaders hate surprises. Guess what? When it comes to what leaders expect of followers, followers hate surprises, too. Therefore, be very specific regarding the outcomes you expect an individual to produce. Help them to set goals, identifying the quantitative and qualitative expectations related to those goals. Prepare them to make the investment of personal and corporate resources—the time, energy, knowledge, and contacts—which will be required for them to pull their weight.

Followers should go into their role fully aware of the mental, physical, emotional, and spiritual expectations that you have of them. If they will require additional training to live up to expectations, they should be cognizant of that investment, too.

Take the time to think through the detailed nature of your expectations and then to discuss those insights with each follower. Some organizations rely upon detailed job descriptions to handle this function, but you should be careful about such written descriptions. Sometimes they become straitjackets that limit rather than clarify what coworkers perceive to be their roles. To avoid this pitfall, know the nature of the person you are leading and craft tools that will work in light of how they process information and direction.

Significance

One of your challenges is not only to describe the vision and resulting consequences in a clear manner but to do so in ways that help each individual feel that his or her role is significant. Nobody wants to wake up every morning to spend the next eight hours doing things that are trivial and forgotten ten minutes later. Everybody wants to feel like their efforts make a difference in the world. Leaders provide that perspective for people.

> *Executives . . . spend nowhere near enough time trying to align their organizations with the values and visions already in place.*
>
> —JIM COLLINS

How well you accomplish that task spells the difference between working with people who are just doing their jobs and those who are agents of positive transformation. Leaders have the ability to think and perceive in this way; most people do not.

Empower your followers by instilling a realistic sense of significance related to them personally and to their work or ministry efforts. Explain to them how what they do matters. Encourage them by providing after-the-fact feedback about the difference their contribution made to the final outcome. Challenge them to be thinking about ways that they can improve and become even more valuable to the cause. Advance their ability to feel pride in their work and in the work of the entire team.

Many leaders get discouraged because they feel that their followers lose interest or do not maintain a consistent level of passion for the vision. Largely this loss of energy and focus relates to how well you tie their sense of personal significance to what you are jointly pursuing. The more you can help them feel a sense of awe regarding the vision (it is, after all, from God!) and to derive pleasure from the fact that they are helping to create something lasting and valuable in service to God, the more comfortable they will be about their role and its significance.[1]

Continuity

Whatever role an individual fills should make use of the resources God invested in that person: intelligence, spiritual gifts, natural talent and ability, learned skills, experiences, education, and so on. To help your followers reach maximum productive capacity, guide them to an understanding of how their background informs and enables them to approach their work in your organization.

Because of the magnitude of God's vision for us, you will often be demanding that people be stretched. It is natural for people to complain about such growing pains because it makes us uncomfortable. This is one way in which the culture you develop will help moderate the levels of moaning and groaning heard among your people. A culture that values personal growth, that identifies discomfort as a possible mark of growth, and that is guided by leaders who are transparent about the tensions that personal development has introduced in their lives but are appreciative for that process is a culture that will grow faster and healthier.

If You Want Good Followers, Create Them

Spirituality

You are not only a leader charged with tangible production, but every leader called by God is expected to be a spiritual leader as well. When challenging your followers to grow, incorporate the spiritual dimension of their development whenever feasible. You may lead in a secular environment in which overt spiritual exhortation is unwise, but there are often opportunities for you to address the intersection of people's spiritual nature and their work. If we are ultimately spiritual beings who live for spiritual purposes, the failure to consider the spiritual side of our work, relationships, perspectives, and outcomes leaves us dangerously and unnecessarily unaware and imbalanced.

In a Ministry Setting

In a church or similar environment, this task is easier but by no means easy. People get involved in churches and other ministries for a variety of reasons, some of which are overtly spiritual, some of which are not. Yet, because the essential thrust of the organization is spiritual, it is easier to raise issues and discuss matters regarding spirituality. As leaders in these situations we should never assume that people are grappling with the spiritual issues related to our joint efforts and purpose; we should intentionally integrate such discussions and thinking into the group dynamics.

In a Business Setting

In a business-oriented setting, the challenges are different. Perhaps you are a Christian in a leadership position, serving in a publicly traded company that produces tangible products—in other words, a place that sells stuff solely to make money. Directing people to recognize the spiritual dimension of their contribution and development will be more difficult but not necessarily impossible, inappropriate, unproductive, or unwanted by your coworkers.

A Fish Out of Water

Our research confirms that seven out of ten adults consider themselves to be "deeply spiritual" and that more than four out of five say their religious faith is very important in their lives. Many people would welcome the chance to consider what their faith has to do with pushing paper or handling customer complaints or filling a slot on the assembly line. What does it have to do with loving God with all our heart, mind, strength, and soul? You can see how such a discussion will invade their area of perceived personal significance. Ordinarily, if such discussions are handled with respect, wisdom, and forethought, they will produce a more engaged workforce and one that appreciates its leaders more deeply, because there is more substance for them to respect. Naturally, such conversations must be sensitive both to the law and to people's interest, but there are more opportunities for such dialogue than we sometimes assume to be the case.

Many individuals do not understand that everything we do is a spiritual act at its core. You do not need to impose your views on everyone to get that across, but as a leader you should have thought through how your faith affects what you do, why you do it, how you do it, and when you will bring this relationship of faith and activity to people's attention. Remember, your role is to develop an empowering culture, which entails helping people interpret and make sense of reality. Avoiding the spiritual dimension of people's contribution to the process diminishes your effectiveness as a leader and their ability to develop a complete understanding and the full benefit of their role.

Developing the Postmodern Follower

Scott, the campaign manager, may not have liked how his boss communicated the need to develop effective followers, but years of hard-won business experience had taught the candidate an important lesson: You cannot be an effective leader unless you have nurtured effective followers. His message to Scott was clear: Leaders don't complain about their situation; they change it. When the issue relates to the capacity of followers to add value in the pursuit of the vision, the question is, What are you doing to help people mature into first-class contributors to the process?

In a postmodern era, where choice, relativism, and process typically prevail over absolutes, truth, and values, the path through which we guide followers may look different than it used to but the ends remain the same. We cannot impose a vision, a life perspective, or a set of values upon people. But we can certainly direct people toward laudable, positive outcomes. Without the old command-and-control approach to leadership, the developmental process takes longer and consumes more resources, but it has longer lasting effects.

Effective leaders these days must roll up their sleeves and become immersed in the messy business of mentoring effective followers. The process involves communicating where you're going, showing them what it takes by revealing the elements of your own journey, helping them to discover their potential within your shared goals, providing them with growth experiences and constructive feedback, and challenging them to continually seek the next stage of personal development within the context of where you are going as a team.

You owe the people on your team respect, fairness, integrity, hope, and the opportunity to grow and succeed. When you deliver these things, your followers are likely to reward you with their best efforts, sincere appreciation, and, perhaps, loyalty. Even in an age of postmodern perspectives, people want to live meaningful and enjoyable lives. You are one of the keys to their ability to do so.

And you need them, too, to have meaning, purpose, and impact in your life. Without followers, you are not a leader, and because there is no bank from which you can simply withdraw great followers, you'll have to grow them. It's part of the bargain that gives you the privilege of leading.

UNCOMFORTABLE QUESTIONS

- Whom are you currently mentoring?

- What percentage of the people in your group or organization do you believe truly understand their role and own it?

- Do you place greater emphasis—judged on the basis of your time and energy investments—on accomplishing tasks, developing ideas and strategies, or growing your people? Is your current allocation of resources correct to accomplish your goal??

- What are the central components of the culture within your organization? How could that culture be changed to increase people's sense of belonging, empowerment, and joy?

—7—

If an individual wants to be a leader and isn't controversial, that means he never stood for anything.

—RICHARD NIXON

Chapter Seven

Conflict: The Leader's Secret Weapon

GENE HAD BEEN A SUCCESSFUL EXECUTIVE at two regional banks prior to accepting the top post at a national financial services firm. His new employer was a fifty-two-year-old company that had become bloated and complacent, with sagging profits and a deteriorating reputation. Wall Street analysts had written off the company as "tired, stodgy, and directionless—not a twenty-first-century player." Employee response to Gene's arrival reflected the ambivalence that permeated the company; many of his employees patronized him, believing that he had no real authority over them and was not likely to be of much help to the firm's waning health. Nevertheless, Gene threw himself into a bridge-building mode during his first half-year on the job, striving to develop genuine relationships within the company and to create a more authentic and widespread sense of community among its several thousand employees.

The new leader was eventually accepted as "a good guy" and was granted some leeway as he spoke to them individually about "coming changes" and the need to take advantage of existing business opportunities that might stretch the company. Gene had performed miracles in his previous positions (the grapevine worked overtime getting the lowdown on the new guy), and he seemed completely self-confident about this approach. However, most employees took a wait-and-see attitude; they'd heard it all before from Gene's predecessors.

On his one-year anniversary, Gene called a companywide meeting. He unveiled a vision statement approved by the board of directors and described changes in executive structure and personnel. The staff was stunned by the magnitude of the changes recommended. Within minutes the response began to emerge.

Some employees were ecstatic about the fresh ideas. They believed this burst of energy would revitalize the company. Others immediately rejected the ideas. They liked things the way they were and had every intention of making Gene's life miserable—and to sink his plan. Still others didn't much care; this was just a job to them, and Gene was simply doing his job, too. They just wanted to know what was expected of them so they could follow the letter of the law and punch out at five.

Even though he was an experienced change agent, Gene was surprised at the degree of resistance his plan met. He summoned all of his energy and charm to persuade the resisters and the complacent, and to use every opportunity to point out the benefits and possibilities his plan represented. For the most part, he made little progress with the intransigents. After many hours of strategic reflection, he chose a bold course of action. He would introduce intentional conflict into the situation, forcing his opponents to one side or the other: either organizational death through refusal to change or potential victory through a willingness to consider options.

His strategy was to subtly but consciously polarize the staff by indicating that out of frustration with their rejection of his initial plan, he was prepared to institute an alternative plan—one that virtually everyone would immediately recognize as an awful alternative. That alternative would include massive labor cutbacks, the elimination of company-paid benefits, and an entirely different customer service system and philosophy.

As expected, the "final option" was roundly rejected by the workforce. In response, Gene chose a leadership group to represent the workforce and imposed a set of ground rules and a deadline regarding the development of a mutually acceptable "final, final option." Gene recognized that this was a risk, but he had hedged his bet by establishing both the parameters of the contest and the nature of an acceptable outcome. He might not get all he felt the company needed at first, but by introducing a plan that generated such intense conflict, he assured himself of something better than what he would have gotten from a face-to-face battle over the original plan. In the end, he was right; he did not get every jot and tittle, but the plan ultimately adopted was viable.

GET USED TO CONFLICT

When Gene accepted the leadership role of the company, he probably did not foresee having to create conflict to make progress. But if he wasn't aware of it before he assumed the leadership, he learned a huge lesson quickly: There's a personal price to pay for executing a vision.

Perhaps the most significant lesson of all, though, was the realization that when you strip it all away, leaders do just two things: They create conflict and they resolve conflict.

I've made that statement at a number of conferences, and people—pastors, especially—are generally stunned by the notion. It's not hyperbole. Leaders create conflict simply by pushing people to focus on God's vision. That creates conflict for most people, because his vision is designed to cause change in our lives—and most people resist change.

Even when particular changes are in our best interest our inclination is to resist, because change implies we are imperfect or somehow lacking. The reality of change is that we must reform our habits, reshape our values, alter our relationships, or adopt new responsibilities. For most of us, that sounds like too much work!

A Fish Out of Water

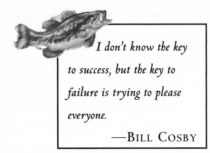

> *I don't know the key to success, but the key to failure is trying to please everyone.*
>
> —Bill Cosby

Given this truism, however, a good leader never seeks change for its own sake or for the adrenaline rush of making things happen. Good leaders realize that change is uncomfortable and approach the necessary activity with courage, compassion, and comprehension.

They have the courage to help us ruthlessly evaluate where we are, why we must change, and what it will take. They demonstrate compassion by empathizing with people's reluctance to change as well as with our unfortunate condition that requires change. They comprehend the reality that leading this process will be painful for everyone involved—including themselves.

Effective leaders always introduce proposed reforms with the promise of helping people resolve the fears, pressures, and issues that are responsible for the resistance. This process is the essence of what leaders do: They identify people's hidden or unspoken failures and then they facilitate the transformations that enhance people's lives. The very changes that bring leaders kudos are based on initially producing pain and discomfort into people's lives.

Of course, conflict is not always instigated by leaders. People have proven their ability to continually stir up conflict without the help of their leaders! Conflict is simply being at odds with the normal state of things; it is a behavior that everybody can and virtually does engage in.

Kinds of Conflict

The most common types of conflict relate to personal issues (personality clashes, power struggles, insecurity, lack of recognition); material issues (fights over property ownership); and ideological or theological differences (differing beliefs). Personal conflict is often an emotional battle; ideological conflict is typically intellectual in its genesis (although it often evolves into an emotional struggle). No matter what type of leadership context you serve in you are likely to encounter each variety of conflict.

To maintain equilibrium and momentum, a leader must recognize when such naturally occurring conflict arises and take steps to address it. Resolution often comes through techniques such as negotiation, establishing dialogue, and empowerment. The failure to adequately deal with internal conflict can paralyze or seriously impair the organization's health, progress, and potential.

In spite of the threat that natural conflict represents, the introduction of controlled and intentional conflict by the leader can be a valuable prod to positive movement and is certainly an underutilized leadership tool.

The remainder of this chapter will focus on conflict intentionally caused by the leader, either through promoting a challenging vision or by undertaking vision-related actions specifically designed to result in productive confrontation. To distinguish it from the tensions and flareups that occur in the normal course of organizational life, let's refer to leader-driven conflict as *strategic conflict.*

> *Sometimes a leader has to draw a line in the sand.*
> —MIKE KRZYZEWSKI,
> *Duke University*

INITIATING STRATEGIC CONFLICT

Although we generally think of conflict in negative terms—as a threat or obstacle—it is just as likely that conflict, especially strategic conflict, represents an opportunity. In fact, wise leaders use conflict to help people grow. It is one of the many tools that they have in their tool kit to make good things happen. When appropriately conceived, initiated, and managed, conflict is a component in a strategic problem-solving approach.

Virtually every healthy organization I have studied has at least one key leader who understands the value and necessity of conflict and uses it as a growth tool.

Don't assume that these are irritating, belligerent people; often, they are easy-going leaders who simply recognize that conflict represents the best option available for moving things forward.

Response by Aptitude

However, it appears that your willingness to integrate conflict depends upon several factors such as personality, emotional stability, spiritual maturity, and leadership aptitude.

Your leadership aptitude is a fairly accurate predictor of how you will deal with conflict. To optimize conflict as a tool, recognize your tendencies and incorporate those inclinations into your planning. In chapter 3 we examined the four leadership aptitudes: the directing, strategic, team-building, and operational types. Let's explore how each type normally handles conflict as a growth tool.

Directing Leaders

Of the four types, directing leaders are the most likely to create tensions for the sake of pushing the group forward. As the dominant vision champion within the leadership team, the directing leader has the most plentiful opportunities to prompt conflict.

In addition, the personality type of most directors lends itself to high-risk behavior—such as intentionally pushing your own people past their prevailing boundaries. While a good leader will never abuse this tactic, directors tend to enjoy the energy, emotional intensity, and change of pace that such tension can promote. Be forewarned, though: After they initiate the conflict and experience the primary benefits to be received, they often delegate the resolution process to others.

Conflict: The Leader's Secret Weapon

Strategic Leaders

Most strategic leaders perceive conflict development to be an intriguing tactic and one whose outcomes are interesting to study. Great strategic leaders are open to any means that will maintain the organization's integrity and spur progress toward the vision. However, introducing external conflict within the group produces internal conflict for strategic leaders. They are generally uncomfortable with high-risk ventures, and they realize that even controlled conflict is never completely predictable.

They may experience another type of internal contradiction, too. As unemotional individuals, they are not terribly concerned about the personal pain of conflict, yet they have an intellectual understanding of the potential price such a tactic could exact from people. In the end, though, their primary interest is in testing different possibilities, observing the results, and drawing conclusions that may help the organization achieve the vision in the present or future situations. They rarely intervene in the process as it is unfolding; they simply collect the pertinent data and interpret the meaning.

Team-Building Leaders

Even under the best of conditions, team-building leaders feel the pain of others. Driven by their heart, it is difficult for team-builders to accept the need for conflict and, yet, because they understand people's emotions, they understand the uses of conflict.

Team-builders generally introduce a different type of conflict than do directors: They often characterize people's choices as undermining an agreed-upon outcome or impairing someone else's ability to accomplish their goals. They may encourage the offender to follow the Matthew 18:15 principle of meeting with the person they have offended and asking forgiveness. When the "offense" is impeding progress toward the vision, the resulting interactions are quite unusual but generally productive.

A Fish Out of Water

Operational Leaders

Operational leaders dislike conflict for two reasons. First, they are often the ones a directing leader calls upon to resolve the issues. Second, as they have a keen interest in maintaining momentum, conflict seems to dampen forward movement with no guarantee of recapturing the spark. Consequently, operational leaders usually want to get the conflict out of the way as quickly and cleanly as possible. On occasion they may introduce conflict of their own volition, but it is not one of the common tricks of the trade they deploy.

Often, they do not get to the root of the problem; they convene the parties involved, conduct a very businesslike reiteration of the matter, and issue a recommended resolution. Once those involved have accepted their recommendation, operationalists refocus people's attention on the tasks at hand.

Conflict on the Team

One of the more interesting ironies is that leadership teams often have an undercurrent of conflict within their team simply by virtue of the emotional and intellectual differences each leader brings to the table. Their divergent ways of gathering and analyzing information, valuing and interacting with people, drawing and implementing conclusions, and communicating with people naturally raise tensions. The element that helps the team to resolve its differences, though, is their common acceptance of the vision as their focus and its efficient pursuit as their goal.

CONFLICT CAN PRODUCE GOOD OUTCOMES

"Conflict is our friend," quipped a pastor at a forum I recently directed. The leaders around the circle laughed at the insider's joke. Those who have a leadership position but lack the stomach for the job smiled politely, unable to savor the irony. How comfortable are you with the idea of using conflict among the people you love and are called to shepherd? If a leader's job is to motivate, mobilize, resource, and direct people to pursue God's vision together, then how might conflict advance that purpose?

> *Consensus means that everybody agrees to say collectively what no one believes individually.*
>
> —ABBA EBAN

Direct Confrontation

As you attempt to motivate people, some will be so distracted by other activities and opportunities that you will need a radical intervention strategy to arrest their attention. Most often, this is done through direct confrontation. You might ask them outright what really matters to them and why there is no evidence that the things of God reign in the hearts. Or, perhaps you will propose a bad idea to shake them out of their lethargy.

Reallocation of Resources

Some followers will upset you because they remain disinterested or dispassionate regarding the vision. In spite of your best efforts to awaken them to the incredible potential and need you face, nothing seems to move them to serious participation. To stir their juices you may need to threaten to reallocate the resources they presently receive—your attention, funding, space, human resources, or other special considerations—in the hope that such a threat will focus them on the vision and its pursuit.

Showing Up Inconsistencies

Sometimes the issue is individuals who won't get with the program because they see things differently and are not willing to compromise. Tactics that often work in those cases include gently caricaturing their position so they can see why their

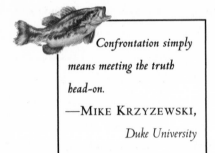

Confrontation simply means meeting the truth head-on.

—MIKE KRZYZEWSKI,

Duke University

way is inferior or how meaningless the distinctions are that prevent them from being part of the team. Imposing deadlines for them to resolve their differences with those they have rejected sometimes forces the issue, too.

When leaders provide direction to their followers, resistance might occur on the basis of ego or in an effort to retain a greater share of power. This is one of the more common weaknesses in followers, stemming from insecurity or selfishness. If more traditional counseling and negotiating practices don't work, direct confrontation regarding their motivations, the inconsistency of their behavior with the values and standards of your group, and the negative outcomes of their behavior might result in a breakthrough.

Peer Pressure

Of course, the most common response to vision is acceptance of the concept but the personal refusal to change. Your goal is to gain universal ownership of the vision. Among those who resist, peer pressure produces tension but also clarifies the stakes and often forces a choice. Leaders sometimes have to go even a step further, continuing to direct people toward the vision while effectively marginalizing the resisters—yet steadfastly offering them a lifeline for involvement and the promise of immediate inclusion in the flow of activity and community life.

BE READY TO DEAL WITH THE CONSEQUENCES

Conflict can be a powerful leadership tool, but it always introduces an element of risk. You must count the cost of this approach and be sure that it is a wise tactic to employ. Using conflict is not appropriate for every situation, and there are some leaders who are not yet mature enough to apply it wisely. In almost every situation I have witnessed, strategic conflict should be a last resort.

Some of your followers will fight your decision to use conflict because they see it as contradicting the biblical principle to love everyone, friend and foe alike. Help them to understand that your purpose is neither to disobey God's commands nor to hurt or denigrate his people. Having exhausted other less-radical options, you are compelled to do what it takes to show them God's love by shaking them to their senses. Strategic conflict is practicing *tough love.*

A harsh reality of leadership is that sometimes you have to be firm and take drastic measures to facilitate dramatic transformation in lives. God's vision calls for us to usher in dramatic transformation; but rest assured it cannot always be accomplished through persuasive talk, developing brilliant strategic plans, and providing organizational structures that pave the way. Often, the resistance we are dealing with is spiritual in nature—that is, supernatural—and must be addressed in a courageous and firm manner.

> *There are always great reasons for cowardice.*
> —KEN FOLLETT

Remember to Pray

The supernatural factor is important to remember. Pray constantly when you lead, particularly when you are taking big risks, and especially when you are instigating conflict for the sake of the vision. Make sure that your prayer is a two-way conversation, allowing God to speak to your mind and heart regarding this tactic. Because of the potential for this approach to backfire, you want to use it only when necessary and only when you feel that God is in the battle with you. But, if my experience is any indicator, this tactic is reasonably at our disposal more often than we imagine.

A FISH OUT OF WATER

Pick Your Battles

Leaders who successfully use this tactic make it work because they have identified

> *The most gifted members of the human species are at their creative best when they cannot have their way.*
> —ERIC HOFFER

their nonnegotiables and fight only for those elements. Great leaders know when to pick worthwhile fights and when to either pull out all the stops or to back off. You cannot fight every battle that emerges on your journey to bringing the vision to fulfillment; you have to pick and choose wisely. Most of the barriers you encounter can be overcome by methods short of conflict and confrontation. Only those that are sufficiently significant to justify the risk and the expense should give rise to strategic conflict.

There are other proven keys to the successful administering of strategic conflict. They include controlling the parameters of the situation (in other words, the rules and guidelines), and launching the process from a position of organizational strength (having a substantial mandate to lead and having widespread public and leadership support). They also involve possessing an unshakeable conviction of your rightness (a stated and demonstrated refusal to concede and an unstated but firmly held willingness to fail) and having the resolve to outlast those who are the source of the hardships.

Three Stages in Conflict

In this last regard, be ready to settle in for a fight, if necessary, since there are generally three stages in any conflict. The first stage is the show (aggressive saber rattling for benefit of others), followed by a period of hard bargaining (probing for opportunities to gain a victory), and finally the conclusion. Conflict research has shown that those who lose the most in conflict make the first and the biggest concessions.

Conflict: The Leader's Secret Weapon

Maybe conflict is not for you—at least, not yet. Always think twice before engaging in strategic conflict—and think even more circumspectly about it if you lack organizational leverage, have a tendency to buckle under stress, are not a competent strategic thinker and planner, or have a low tolerance for ambiguity and uncertainty. Most people can upgrade their skills and their capacity to use strategic conflict to the advantage of their team, but it takes both desire and effort to grow in this competency.

DON'T NEGLECT CONFLICT

Leaders who use conflict as a growth tool get a reputation for being controversial and "in your face." If that characterization facilitates your pursuit of God's vision, run with it! Tom Peters has helped many organizations by making extreme statements and allowing the organization's devotees to push back until they have arrived at an optimal position. Peter Drucker has spent six decades brilliantly staring down the myths that prevail in corporate America. Lyle Schaller has made a career of helping churches to see themselves more accurately by putting the raw truth on the table and guiding them as they address what's there. Pat Riley did not become one of the winningest coaches in basketball history by smiling and patting every player on the back; he has confronted a lot of issues that ultimately led to stronger and more productive teams.

You should not overuse this tool, of course. But if you hit an impasse and other techniques and strategies are not producing results, consider a dose of conflict. After you identify the obstacle to progress, consider how conflict might break up the logjam. Give it some time to unfold, watch it carefully, shape its development, and make your move to resolve the tension at the appropriate moment. You do not want to introduce conflict that will hurt people, only that which will help them and the group you're leading.

UNCOMFORTABLE QUESTIONS

- What are the limitations you have established regarding your use of conflict to accomplish desired outcomes?
- Have you recently compromised your position on a significant issue because you did not want to offend an important constituency? In retrospect, do you feel that the avoidance of conflict in that situation was the best course of action?
- How well do you assess people's fears and concerns before injecting conflict into a situation?
- How often do you initiate strategic conflict?
- Would you be a more effective leader if you introduced strategic conflict more frequently?

—8—

> *Other qualifications for spiritual leadership are desirable. To be Spirit-filled is indispensable.*
>
> —J. Oswald Sanders

CHAPTER EIGHT

God First, Leadership Second

AVID WAS THE SENIOR PASTOR of a thriving church in a major metropolitan area. His congregation appreciated his leadership, biblical scholarship, and practical approach to ministry and life. But after twenty-three years at the helm, he was feeling distracted and restless. Through a series of unusual circumstances, he decided to take a big risk and accepted the pastorate of a small, stagnant church some fourteen hundred miles away. With many tears but no regrets, he turned over the leadership to the associate whom he had hired a dozen years earlier and had mentored ever since. His parting sermon and the send-off afterward left not a dry eye in the house, including David's.

He arrived at his new ministry after a week of vacation and a week of moving. He found his new congregants to be welcoming and optimistic, but there was no doubting the fact that the church was terminally stagnant. It would take a miracle to turn the ministry around—and that's exactly what David was expecting and what God had in mind for the tiny ministry outpost.

Energized by this imposing challenge, the revived pastor dove into the situation and vigorously attacked the multitude of barriers confining the church. He spent time working on a vision for the church. He recruited and trained lay leaders. He reorganized the staff and church structure. He eliminated several dead programs while introducing a serious prayer ministry. He continued to devote substantial time to sermon preparation, and he even led a Sunday school class. One of his great joys was playing the guitar in the worship band, a practice that the plethora of good musicians at his previous church had precluded. As daunting as the challenge was, David felt alive spiritually and had a sense of joy unlike any he had experienced in the past several years. He knew he was where God wanted him to be.

Seven years later, the fruit of David's efforts was unmistakable. The congregation had exploded from seventy-four people his first week in town to an average of more than five hundred showing up each week. They were immersed in a multimillion-dollar capital campaign to renovate the dilapidated buildings and expand the worship center. It seemed as if a new ministry was started every month, and even the previously dormant youth program was attracting kids from all over the area.

But this "success" was redefining not only the church but David as well. It wasn't an ego problem; he gave the credit to God and was totally focused on developing the church. The problem was his own spiritual growth.

He had put it on hold while he juggled the church's expanding needs and opportunities. He no longer spent hours each week preparing sermons that also stretched him spiritually; he was resigned to recycling the sermons from his prior pastorate. He surrendered the teaching of the Sunday school because of the inability to prepare each week. His guitar-playing days were through, too; it was all he could do to be sure he was ready to deliver his message without taking on worship rehearsals. Family issues also arose, as his kids were in high school and wanted him to be at their games. He also had to rework his schedule to ensure regular time with his wife, who felt abandoned as Dave devoted himself to the church.

David finally worked up the courage to raise the issue with the three local pastors he met for breakfast every couple of weeks. One asked David about the nature of his relationship with God and how he nurtured that tie each day.

A chill ran down David's spine as the question was asked. He was silent for a few moments before giving a perfunctory response about his time in the Word, his prayer life, and other marks of spiritual health. It was his last comment during their breakfast that morning. His mind raced with the realization that for several years he had been revving up the organizational motor and had it running full speed. But personally, he was running on fumes. He had failed to keep refueling his tank.

David knew it was only a matter of time before there was nothing left to give and his race would be over. What worried him the most was that he may even have reached that point already but was simply too busy to notice. He finally realized that the lack of joy he was feeling was attributable to his obsession with what he was doing, rather than whom he was becoming. Although he was helping the church to do what churches do, he was making no time to grow the relationship with the God he was allegedly serving.

BEING A LEADER WHO IS CHRISTIAN

David experienced spiritual depletion as a pastor. I know people—and I'm sure you do, too—who are working themselves to the bone in leadership, trying to show what Christian leadership looks like, but are struggling because they are spiritually spent or distracted. It is never a pretty sight to behold, and yet it happens all the time.

We Americans are so caught up in being *on the edge* and achieving *success* that sometimes we lose sight of where the real edge is or what the ultimate goal is. We become so seduced by the goodies and applause of the world and so mesmerized by the competition to attain those things that we forget we are spiritual people who live for a spiritual purpose.

Leadership is simply one expression of your Christian-ness. Your calling and ability to lead are much less important to the God who created you than is your determination to know him deeply and love him every moment of your life. Because of your reliance upon Jesus Christ for your continued relationship with him, God cares deeply and eternally about you—not about your performance statistics, your creative ideas, or your groundbreaking methods. He created you so that he could love you and be loved by you. If you can foster that passion through acts of leadership, wonderful. But he is not interested in leadership done in his name that comes without a wholehearted commitment to himself. Leading people without a continual, authentic love affair with God is empty and legalistic. It may impress the world, but it does not impress God. Leading without an intimate relationship with the Lord becomes toxic; his presence and loving involvement in your life is the air that a Christian, and especially a Christian leader, must breathe to survive.

This, then, is one of the paradoxes of Christian leadership: The excellence of your leadership depends more on the quality of your relationship with God than on the application of the gifts and resources he has given to you for success in leading people.

> *Jesus has established the model for Christian leaders. It is not found in His "methodology." Rather, it is seen in His absolute obedience to the Father's will.*
> —HENRY BLACKABY

Have you ever stopped to wonder what is the difference between a leader who is Christian and a leader who is not? In its simplest form, the answer is that a leader who is Christian surrenders to the Holy Spirit; a leader who is not, does not. But in practical terms, what does that mean for a Christian who feels called by God to lead?

God First, Leadership Second

Clues to What Makes a Difference

To understand how God might answer that question, revisit the Book of Acts. What you will discover in that narrative is a group of followers of Christ who lived in the world but not according to the world; they sold out to God. They were committed to living in harmony with what they understood Jesus to have taught, modeled, and exhorted.

In short, they took hold of six pillars of the faithful life. They knew they needed to understood the challenge to

- worship God constantly with reverence, purity, intensity, and sincerity;
- study God's Word tirelessly so it would saturate our hearts and thereby shape all our thoughts and behavior;
- share our faith in Jesus Christ joyfully with everyone who does not know him personally and intimately as Savior;
- utilize the resources God entrusts to us strategically as stewards investing in his kingdom;
- serve anyone humbly who has needs, particularly those who are emotionally, physically, intellectually, or spiritually disadvantaged; and
- develop a loving community of believers who would encourage, exhort, and support each other as fellow members of the household of God.

We have the same mandate today. Every leader who is Christian is a disciple of Jesus, first and foremost. As disciples of Christ, we are to commit ourselves to worship, spiritual formation, evangelism, stewardship, community service, and community among believers so that we might be the true church that Jesus came to earth to establish—and that he died to advance. Whether you are a habitual leader or a situational leader, you will not be a *Christian* leader unless you have a life-changing relationship with Jesus and devote yourself to the constant pursuit of these six pillars of the faithful life.

The dilemma regarding this message is that you've heard it all before and are probably immune to this challenge. I don't say that to be unkind; I suffer from

A Fish Out of Water

> *While cultures, methods, and technologies change, the key to touching people timelessly for eternity has not changed. Ultimately, it is done in living out "the basics."*
>
> —JACK HAYFORD

the same numbness to this repeated message. After all, how many lessons have we endured that instructed us to live Christianly so that we could lead like Christ? How many books have communicated about being a Christlike leader by allowing what he has done in you to flow out of you? In a nation that thrives on sound bites, demands the latest and most exciting possibilities, and has an attention span of less than ten minutes, what chance does any messenger have of riveting your focus on the need to put God first and foremost?

And yet, that's the heart of the entire game. Unless the Holy Spirit guides your mind, your heart, and your body every moment, and you are devoted to knowing and being with God such that he has the opportunity to refine you into Christlikeness, you're just acting. And actors do not make good leaders. What people get from an actor is a reflection of something that is real and substantive, not the real thing.

If God has called you to lead, and you want to honor him through your leadership, then you must be in hot pursuit of God.

As a leader, you cannot give what you do not have; and as a *Christian* who leads, if what you have is not from God and of God, what you give isn't worth getting. On the other hand, the more you grow in the depth and breadth of your relationship with him, the more of value and substance you have to give, and the more desirable and significant your leadership becomes.

It Can Dry Up

As Pastor David discovered, even if you had a tight bond with God that enabled you to grow deep in him and provide people with serious guidance, that well can dry up over time. The relationship with God cannot be something you invested in at one point in time, like a graduate school degree, to add value, open doors, and provide sufficient long-term capacity. As time progresses, leaders give more and more of themselves to people, and people grow as a result of that investment. But circumstances change and your reserves get depleted. What you used to have in order to give ceases to be both available and appropriate in the new circumstances. Unless you stay fresh and renewed, you lose your value to those who rely upon leaders for direction.

We will never be perfect or righteous on our own, but effective leaders are those who keep things in perspective and have their priorities straight. You are leading in the midst of a raging spiritual battle; the last thing you want to do is shed your spiritual armor and ammunition, even for "just a season," while the battle rages on around and within you. Perhaps the single most important quality that you can direct people to pursue—and it is always the bedrock underlying the visible manifestation of God's vision—is an obsession with being obedient to God and living a holy life.

THE LEADER AS WORSHIPER

If the role of a leader is to give people appropriate cues to follow, then you must ask what kind of worship leader you are. By *worship leader* I do not mean the individual who guides a congregation's singing and prayers on Sunday mornings. You must show people what worship looks like in real life, outside of the sanctuary. Your leadership is an act of worship, and by following your lead, people should be brought into the presence of God more deeply and consistently.

Desperately Seeking God

God is seeking leaders who are desperate for intimacy with him. King David was an effective leader not because of his education (he had little) or lineage, but

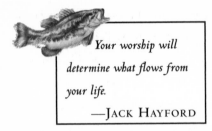

> *Your worship will determine what flows from your life.*
>
> —JACK HAYFORD

because of his determination to love God to the utmost. David was one of the great God worshipers in history. His passion to experience a connection with God changed his life—and God has changed the lives of millions of people through David's worshipful witness. The prophet Samuel, speaking for the Lord, put his finger on the reason when he informed Saul that he was being removed as king because God had found David to be "a man after [God's] own heart."[1] The same desperation that Jacob demonstrated by wrestling with God to gain his blessing is the type of desperation and persistence that God looks for from his appointed leaders today.[2]

Unfortunately, my research regarding worship has shown that most of us relegate worship to the one hour each week we join together in the sanctuary at church. How disappointed God must be by our decision to worship him for just one hour a week! In the Bible we are instructed to make worship a lifestyle, not an isolated event. We should seek opportunities to worship him corporately and privately, with our family as well as our coworkers and friends. We may not break out in song in the marketplace, as the apostles did, or dance frenetically in public as King David did, but different forms of praise are possible in every venue in which we find ourselves.

Worship on the Brain

To become a leader who evokes worship requires us to have *worship on the brain*— that is, to be ever vigilant in spotting opportunities to express praise, adoration, gratitude, and respect to the Father. Our objective is to glorify God at all times—through everything that we think, say, and do. To arrive at that state of mind we must develop an understanding of God and a relationship with him that is based on trust, gratitude, fear, and love—an odd combination of factors, but these core attributes give evidence of our true feelings and desires.

Not long ago we conducted a two-year study of worship in America. We learned that most Christians, including both clergy and laity, struggle with the practice of worship. Millions of regular churchgoers say they have never felt that they experienced God's presence during worship services (or elsewhere) and that the notion of interacting with the living God is unfathomable.

Obstacles to Genuine Worship

Among the obstacles to genuine worship were these: not having been been taught the purpose and practice of worship and consequently substituting a series of rituals for connection with God; assuming that learning about God is good enough, without actually interacting with him; and ignoring or suppressing the leading of the Holy Spirit in order to maintain our dignity or focus on matters other than worship. Other factors were overlooking the necessity of regularly confessing our sins so that we might enter the presence of a holy and righteous God; and becoming so comfortable with our forgiving, loving, and merciful God that we lack a sense of awe and fear that will drive our desire to glorify him.

How's your worship life? Unless you have a rich experience of God's presence on a regular basis, and delve into genuine episodes of praising him every day, you are missing out on one of the phenomenal opportunities of your lifetime. That absence of a worshipful life will also limit your capacity to influence others for God. To lead people toward fulfilling God's vision, help them to be in his presence day after day. You can only do that if you're already there.

THE LEADER AS DISCIPLE

We love shortcuts. Against our better judgment we even try to shortcut our way to spiritual maturity. By definition, though, there are no such shortcuts; spiritual maturity is a process of going deep in your relationship with God and being able to lead others onto a similar journey. Reading the Bible, reflecting on devotional texts, praying—these are good and useful practices, but they do not necessarily constitute a regimen that produces a true disciple.

Making Discipleship a Priority

Another multiyear research project we recently completed focused on discipleship. As was true regarding worship, we found that most Christians are not very committed to spiritual depth; just one out of five makes spiritual growth a top personal priority. While the figure was higher among leaders, a minority of Christians who hold positions of leadership or are called and gifted as leaders deem serious discipleship to be a high goal in their life.

> Our concern must be to enlarge our acquaintance, not only with the doctrine of God's attributes, but with the living God whose attributes they are.
>
> —J. I. PACKER

Here are some of the obstacles we discovered:

- a lack of goals for their growth,
- the absence of accountability for growth,
- confusing genuine maturation with mere exposure to teaching, and
- a limited emotional and time investment in growth activities.

Effective leadership is dependent on credibility and trust. What kind of consistency do people sense between who you are and what you strive to achieve? Every Christian who is called to lead should be committed to continual spiritual growth. Your life is an external representation of your internal nature; the inner nature needs constant shaping and sharpening to honor God and represent him well. How are you doing in your becoming a laudable imitation of Christ?

God First, Leadership Second

THE LEADER AS EVANGELIST

One of the common reactions of Christians is that they do not need to engage in evangelism because it is not their gift. The reality is that God expects all of his people—and especially leaders—to reach out with the good news about what he has done for all people. Being open to personal involvement in evangelism is not a matter of receiving supernatural ability to proselytize; rather, it is an issue of heartfelt gratitude for an undeserved gift of eternal life and a willingness to share that gift with other undeserving people.

Fear of Rejection and Other Excuses

Our surveys among leaders who are Christian revealed some disturbing trends. Only about half of the nation's leaders who are Christian share their faith in Christ with others, and those who do so share infrequently. The chief reasons are the fear of rejection or being labeled a religious zealot; lack of preparation to defend or explain the Christian faith; not having serious relationships with non-Christian people, which allow such conversations to develop; concern about being viewed as inappropriately using their leadership position to promote Christianity; and not caring enough about the souls of others to make the effort to share the gospel.

Good arguments can be made to defend each of these reasons for squelching the gospel—good, that is, until you ponder whether those arguments would impress God. Every leader has a different story to tell regarding his or her path to Christ and eternal life; that story is an important tale that needs to be told. Because of the profile and wealth of human contacts that leaders have, remaining sensitive

> *No earthly enterprise is as important as the business of bringing lost people to the cross of Christ. This should be central to the lives of all of His followers, regardless of what they do for a career.*
>
> —BILL HYBELS

to opportunities to tell that story and answer people's questions about God and faith is a crucial determinant of your effectiveness as a leader.

One hundred years from now, nobody will remember that you hit your profit goals or organized the neighborhood watch or recruited a record number of volunteers. What will remain are the souls that live in God's presence because you were bold enough and prepared enough to tell people about Jesus. You cannot convert people—that's the job of the Holy Spirit—but God relies on those he has saved to bring others along for the ride. Leaders have more opportunities than most people to make those life-saving connections. And, of course, with greater opportunity comes greater responsibility.

Do you think of your leadership as an impediment to sharing your faith or a door opener? Of course, you should share your faith at appropriate times among appropriate people, and do so with sensitivity—but one of the reasons why God has you in a leadership capacity is to spread his holy name and compassionate works to those who need to know.

THE LEADER AS STEWARD

If you are a vocational leader—a business person, minister, nonprofit executive, school administrator, or the like—your performance is probably evaluated on the basis of how well you account for your organization's resources. God has a similar expectation of you. As one of his chosen leaders, you are to identify, organize, and allocate the entire parcel of resources he has entrusted to you to achieve his desired outcomes. Those resources include time, money, relationships, ideas, and power.

God is wonderfully generous and expects us to enjoy the bounty of resources he gives us access to; all he asks is that we utilize those resources in ways that fit his principles and facilitate his outcomes. Once again, as his appointed one you have the chance to show people how a Christian gains joy by serving God, even through your handling of material and nonmaterial assets.

Leaders sometimes stumble in this area because they lack balance in perspective and performance. We are often compensated above the norm. We may be blessed with an abundance of creative ideas, which then attract attention, money, and more opportunities. We have problem-solving skills which open many doors for us and reap plentiful rewards. These advantages and resulting benefits are to be enjoyed but are also to be held in balance: We deserve none of the benefits, but we may choose to receive and distribute those as we see fit. How wisely do you pass along the assets over which you rule?

THE LEADER AS CAREGIVER

One of the fundamental lessons of Christianity is that if you wish to be made whole, then you must get your eyes off of yourself and onto other people. Jesus' leadership was a perfect model of this: His time and energy were spent on two elements—knowing God and serving people. Just as God makes good on his promise to take care of us by bringing other people into our life who nurture and support us, he relies upon us to be his means of compassionate assistance to other people. Some of those will be people we know well, some will be passing acquaintances, others will be complete strangers—but they are all God's children and he expects us to love them to the best of our abilities.

God's vision is about developing a preferable future for people. Look around your church, your place of business, your family, your neighborhood, and your community. In each of those venues you can probably identify at least one or two serious dilemmas that require attention. Each of those demands leadership to experience and sustain progress. The Lord has graciously given each of us a menu of opportunities to choose from.

But the challenge is not simply to identify those opportunities and send others out, but for you and me to choose an area of service, roll up our sleeves, and jump in the trenches to do the work of loving and helping the helpless. Jesus identified the options as serving the poor, the sick, the lonely, the imprisoned, and children.[3] There are plenty of opportunities to go around!

> *We are sent into the world, like Jesus, to serve. For this is the natural expression of our love for our neighbors. We love. We go. We serve. . . . Love has no need to justify itself. It merely expresses itself in service wherever it sees need.*
>
> —JOHN STOTT

What group of people has needs that penetrate the inner recesses of your heart? How are you helping them? Perhaps you are able to apply your leadership abilities to their plight. Even if you serve without leading, that act of sacrifice and compassion will bolster your capacity to lead with authenticity and passion.

The Leader As Friend

We are immersed in the battle of our lives. Satan has declared war against God and his people. Everyone is on one side or the other; there are no innocent bystanders in this spiritual battle, for everyone is either with God or against God. As Christians who have been called into leadership, we are engaged in acts of warfare every day. It will be a fight to the finish.

In war, one of the few great comforts is having others on your side you can confide in, receive assurance and understanding from, and enjoy being with. War is depleting; it takes everything out of you. How refreshing it is to be able to spend time in the company of those who not only share the burden of the battle but also the privilege of uplifting each other in-between battlefield confrontations.

Your fellow believers are those supportive troops. Whether it be at your church, in a small group, through a lunchtime meeting of believers at work, or participation in a Christian sports league or hobby club, you need to be connected to God's people in some discernible and regular way. Friendship with other believers provides opportunities for emotional renewal, spiritual encouragement, personal accountability, and enjoyment of God's creation.

It is not uncommon for leaders to get so wrapped up in the battle that we forfeit the value of spending time relaxing and having fun with others who are engaged in the battle as well. The absence of relationships with like-hearted people robs us of the internal resuscitation that gut-wrenching, labor-intensive spiritual warfare demands. Sometimes we take ourselves so seriously and worry so much about our ability to lead effectively that we fail to loosen up and get close to people, fearing that such vulnerability will undermine our leadership.

Who are your friends within the body of Christ? How often do you let loose with them and just enjoy a frivolous and refreshing experience with them?

NO EXCUSES

God called you to leadership, not perfection, but he expects each of us, regardless of our gift and calling to invest ourselves in the pursuit of spiritual maturity. The more complete we become in Christ, the more effective we will be in taking the point on the march toward his vision for us. Unless we are continually growing in our faith and the outworking of our faith, though, we lose the spiritual edge that serves as the point in our efforts to penetrate the world's darkness.

A Balanced Christian

Our research reveals that people's tendency is to focus on working hard to grow in one or two of the six pillars. That creates an imbalanced Christian. Because you pass on what you are, it means that leaders often produce followers who are similarly imbalanced. It also leaves us inadequately prepared to lead from a position of strength; our spiritual weaknesses inevitably limit our influence for Christ and the wholeness of what emerges from our leadership efforts.

You can no more hope to lead effectively while putting your personal spiritual development on the back burner for a while any more than a marksman can hope to maintain his precision without regular target practice or an athlete can hope to maintain a rigorous training schedule without the benefit of eating. Evaluate

> *So the leader rises out of the Jordan and walks out of the desert, knowing that his priorities are to hear God's Word, worship God's greatness, await God's time.*
>
> —LEIGHTON FORD

yourself regularly and honestly in regard to the six pillars—worship, spiritual knowledge and application, evangelism, stewardship, community service, and fellowship with believers—and intentionally pursue growth in each of those areas. The growth will not come without a cost, but your effort will ensure that you have something of value to give and the strength with which to wage the good fight of faith.

UNCOMFORTABLE QUESTIONS

- How many days last week did you take time to consciously worship God?
- What are your personal goals for learning more about your faith this year, and what plan have you crafted to facilitate meeting those goals?
- With whom are you currently developing a relationship in the hope of being able to share your faith in Christ at some future time?
- How could you be using God's resources more effectively to advance his kingdom?
- What impact have you made in the lives of disadvantaged people during the past year because of the time and energy you gave to serving those people?
- How often do you get together with fellow Christians for times of fun and relaxation, forgetting your position and simply kicking back to enjoy their presence?

— 9 —

> *As the organization changes in its life cycle, different styles of leadership are needed.*
>
> —ICHAK ADIZES

CHAPTER NINE

What Got You Here Won't
Get You Where You Need to Go

AMES STARTED HIS AD AGENCY twelve years ago. He had previously worked for two other agencies but had left the last one during a corporate downsizing period before the ax found his neck. Thus the launching of his one-man show. It wasn't long, though, before his skill as a salesman landed his first client, causing him to add staff. The agency was built on some novel ideas about media use and the integration of marketing research into advertising and product-positioning decisions. James had never thought of himself as entrepreneurial, but once he got in that mode he thrived in it.

The company grew slowly but steadily. The first five years were difficult: Cash flow was a constant noose around the agency's neck, and every other Friday (in other words, payday) brought a wave of panic over him as he examined the bank balance. Year six brought the breakthrough the agency needed, though, with when a major cable television network signed on as a client, followed shortly by a second cable network. Now the agency was on the map. James was able to breathe a bit easier, although it seemed he had to work even harder to maintain the new level of activity.

A FISH OUT OF WATER

Sustaining and developing the company proved to be even more taxing on James than building from nothing. The more he talked with peers in the industry the more he realized that his agency was entering a new level that required a different blend of leadership talents.

When the firm was a start-up, and even in its more stable postconception years, James kept things going by force of will, passion, and countless hours. What he said was what was done; he had control and his team was too busy to fight his dictates. His fellow leaders deferred to him in almost every case. Now, however, he was struggling to adapt to a new role in which he was not always the central decision maker and sometimes did not even understand what his appropriate role might be. There were days he didn't want to go to the office.

He wasn't alone. Although his coworkers liked and appreciated James, they were often frustrated at the decision-making process. *We'll do it as soon as James croaks or strokes* became a phrase used behind his back, suggesting that until he died or retired to the golf course, the maturing so desperately needed was not likely to happen.

Meanwhile, the agency became chaotic. It was no longer enough to send James out to sell while the rest of the team stayed at the office and produced quality advertising. Its growth had led to inefficiency, there was a dearth of planning, systems were missing, and people were moving in multiple directions at once. What had gotten James and the agency to where it stood was not what it needed to get to the next level of health and growth.

Finally, the board of directors—of which James was chairman—called a meeting to confront the issue. In diplomatic language James's fellow board members made their message clear to him: *Move over or move out.*

At first bewildered, then angry, James felt like the target of a benign coup. His partners explained that the decision was not personal. The founder of the agency was still working long hours and doing what he did best, but what he did best was no longer what the agency needed most from its primary leader. Survival required forms of growth that James had not instituted, and now the agency and everyone in it was suffering because of his limitations. The board made it clear it was not pushing him out; it simply wanted him to partner more effectively with other qualified and passionate leaders within the firm—those who had leadership abilities that better fit the current needs of the organization.

It was time to rethink what leadership meant at the agency—and how James could best contribute to the future of the firm he had started.

PAYING ATTENTION TO LIFE CYCLES

Every living organism experiences life cycles. People typically move from conception to infancy, adolescence, early adulthood, married life, parenthood, the empty nest, retirement, and widowhood. In each phase we experience new challenges and develop new skills. The failure to progress at any stage hampers our ability to flourish in the next stage. As we age we have to learn how to handle greater complexity, pressures, and expectations; how to assess our situations accurately and make better decisions about resources; and how to anticipate changes required to move on to the next stage of life. If we don't, we jeopardize our health and fulfillment, as well as that of the people and organizations that rely upon us.

The same is true for organizations and their leaders. I believe organizations pass through six stages:

- conception
- infancy
- expansion
- balance
- stagnation
- disability

The first two stages are developmental: The foundations are being created that will determine the potential of the organization. The middle two phases are

> *It is one of the major disservices of the "superman" school of leadership that it suggests a leader can command all situations with the same basic gifts.*
>
> —GARRY WILLS

the growth stages during which the organization expands its influence and establishes stability. The final two, which we want to avoid, are the stages of decline. This pattern holds true whether the organization is a for-profit business, a nonprofit charitable organization, a church, a government agency, or an educational institution. It is also relevant to organizations regardless of their size or sophistication: IBM and Disney are as beholden to this pattern as are Bible study groups and Sunday school classes.

As you might imagine, a key factor in enabling an organization to enter the growth and stability stages and avoid the decline phases is the leadership provided. An organization can go no further than its leader can take it. It reflects the health quotient of its leader. Consequently, unless a leader is competent to direct the fortunes of the group through the phase in which it resides, the trajectory toward decline is hastened, and the potential that may have existed dissipates.

The natural tendency for any organization as it ages is to avoid risk. Procedures become more rigid and confining, courage begins to wane, success brings complacency and comfort, and the vision seems less compelling. The only way to sidestep this state is to *jump the curve*, which we'll talk about more fully later, and to re-energize the process with new ideas and initiatives that reinvigorate and re-engage people in the work. Knowing when and how is a leadership responsibility.

THE SIX PHASES

Let's examine the six phases and the types of leadership needed to maintain maximum health and impact.

Conception

This is an exciting time for an organization's founder and those who buy into the vision. It is a period marked by the birthing of ideas, the assessment of personal strengths and marketplace needs, and intense dialogue among the group's zealots as they try to answer *why* the organization they are birthing is needed in today's world.

Emotions run high as the founding group puts things in place prior to its official launch. In its haste to prepare for impact, and energized by the potential and internal zeal, unrealistic promises are often made regarding likely productivity and influence. Sheer enthusiasm and energy, combined with the group's responsiveness to a perceived need and its practical competence, create momentum for the launch.

Leadership in the infancy stage consists of balancing several archetypes: dreamer, prophet, champion, entrepreneur, founder, and producer. The dominant question that the leader answers throughout the conception phase is why anyone should be excited about what the organization will produce.

Every leader is a juggler, but the elements juggled vary by phase. In this initial stage leaders juggle a little bit of everything, often striving single-handedly to keep every ball in the air simultaneously. They're the *jack of all trades, master of none.* It is their ideas and versatility in support of the core concept that get the organization off the ground.

This has both a positive and a negative side. On the plus side is the fact that these leaders have created something from nothing: They have leveraged energy and ideas into a tangible product or service desired by enough people to sustain the growth of a larger—perhaps even profitable or influential—organization. The minus side of the ledger reflects the internal chaos, lack of capacity and resources, and unrealistic perspectives that usually characterize the group.

The leadership aptitude that dominates the scene in a start-up is the directing aptitude. Such a person's ability to pump people up regarding the central concept (in other words, vision) without getting bogged down in details is integral to breathing life into a still-conceptual organism. In fact, the perfectionism and realism of the strategic leader, the time-consuming networking and broad focus of the team-builder, and the systems thinking of the operational leader may threaten the director's sense of momentum, urgency, and exhilaration. The directing leader is often high on the vision and doesn't want the "pessimists" and other foot draggers to spoil the party.

Infancy

Once the organization officially launches, entirely new challenges arise. The emphasis shifts from vision casting and motivation to production and sustenance. Instead of answering the question, *Why do you need to exist?* the primary question to answer becomes, *What do you have that I need?* If the organization is a business, there must be sufficient sales and timely delivery of products; if it's a church, then attendance and giving are the indicators of interest; nonprofits watch contributions and how clientele is served; schools focus on tuition income and student enrollment, and so forth. Structure must be introduced to enable the organization to be minimally efficient and productive.

Still founder-dependent, the group is now in a high sales mode, reflecting frenetic activity to generate public interest and satisfy demand, while somehow producing enough to keep the whole operation going and growing. During this phase, the pressure to grow quickly enough causes unrealistic commitments to its constituency. Internal chaos reigns: People are more conscious of production and sustainability than policies, procedures, rules, roles, and systems. The quality level may be spotty, but the mere fact that there is finally a tangible product is paramount. The assumption is that once the group establishes a foothold in its marketplace, then it will have the luxury of enhancing quality through superior systems and quality control.

The pressure to produce mandates huge personal sacrifices, resulting in long hours for little remuneration. What keeps the passion and energy high is the sense that the vision can be realized, whether through profit, promotions, and megasalaries, souls saved, lives changed, or a renewed culture. The focus is still on the future; the motivation remains the promise of future payoffs. The urgent need around which the troops rally, however, is building a stable foundation on which a larger and more influential entity can be built. Cash flow or, more accurately, lack thereof—is the enemy that precipitates the crisis.

The strategic leader is dominant in this phase. The primary leader shifts from one who is a dreamer to one who is a producer. The ability to convert the founding vision into practical plans for a skeletal workforce is pivotal to survival. Authority and decision making are centralized in this phase to maintain tight control over costs and actions. The skills of the strategist fuel early growth, but the abilities of the directing leader are also vital to making the shoestring operation a place that hums with high expectations and a sense of ability to do the impossible.

Expansion

Growth is the name of the game in this phase. The emphasis moves from gross sales to net profit because finally there is some profit to measure. For ministries, the equation might be shifting from increased attendance to significant ministry output. The key question the organization must answer shifts this time to, *How will we manage our growth and meet our goals most efficiently?*

The continued expansion is a result of greater understanding of, and responsiveness to the needs of the marketplace. In this phase the organization responds to opportunities rather than creates them. They have been around long enough for people to recognize they need what the group has to offer.

However, the success of the organization starts to go to its head during this time. Often, the group starts to feel invincible and thus launches out in too many directions to be effective. People still lack the tools to do the job at its highest level, and the growth puts on the organization new pressures it has never had to deal with before.

A FISH OUT OF WATER

During this period, the leadership is stretched to capacity. More people are invited into the leadership circle, but few are ready for the challenges that rapid growth introduces. Intelligent delegation is often at a premium. By necessity, power and authority start to be decentralized, but this also raises considerable internal conflict and discomfort. Even the founder—if he or she is still around—feels threatened during this stage, as the organization seems to pass by at ninety miles per hour.

Team-building and operational leaders ascend. This is the first stage at which the operational and team-building leaders must assume a larger share of the burden. The swift change and inconsistency that characterizes this stage demands the steadying hand and systems approach of the operationalist. Introducing systems, policies, and predictable decision making offers some sense of stability and logic to the organization. Meanwhile, the swirl of activity requires deft recruiting and deployment of human resources, which is the forte of the team builder. The influx of people and opportunities is evidence that the directing leader has adequately cast the vision and motivated people to buy in. The strategic leader is still mired in analyzing and planning but relying more heavily on the operational and team-building leaders to run with the directives.

Balance

This is ultimately where you want to land. It is that exhilarating time in an organization's history when the engine is running on all eight cylinders. Growth is continuing but at a reasonable pace (which for churches is generally in the 12 to 15 percent range regarding attendance—less impedes optimization, more kills you). The systems introduced in the preceding phase start to take root and produce both efficiency and effectiveness. The vision has become an integral aspect of the group's culture and a recognized mark of the organization. Productivity (your quantitative output) and performance (the quality of your productivity) are above average. Having answered the questions regarding why you exist, what you produce, and how you can make a go of it, your big question in this phase is, *Where do we go from here?*

All four leaders guide. In a state of balance, all four of your leaders are sharing the load. Each one is now riveted by specific challenges their unique aptitude equips them to address. The directing leader may be torn between keeping people focused on the primary vision and conceptualizing a new horizon to chase. The strategic leader is balancing analysis and evaluation of the present condition with an exploration of alternative adventures for the organization to consider. The team builder is juggling people's excitement from success with declining morale of no longer being part of a small, intimate community and having lots of attention. The operational leader is striving to perfect the corporate culture while also examining options for heightening efficiency.

During this period an organization often will spin off new groups (such as new churches, sister businesses). It is also a time when some of your most talented colleagues will jump ship because they realize they are no longer (or never were) paramount in the stream of activity and would prefer to play a more central role in another organization. Maintaining the stability and health of the leadership ranks is one of the great challenges during this otherwise blessed stage.

Stagnation

Too much of a good thing often makes organizations complacent. Like people, they can get lazy, fat, and arrogant. The result is a stagnant operation: The vision is central but the passion is missing. Happy with how things are going, the organization stops taking risks. There is a power shift that happens internally. Leaders become caretakers, and the most listened-to individuals are the accountants and financial managers. Instead of seeking new hills to take, the mind-set becomes protectionist: The group starts getting defensive rather than aggressive, hoping to protect what it has rather than winning what it could have.

The deeper the organization gets in this mode, the more the mind-set gets set in stone. Entirely new forms of behavior enter in: greater formality in relationships and operations, less appreciation for new ideas and creative solutions, a flurry of self-preserving memos and paperwork, general detachment from the vision and grand outcomes, and rising control issues. In this stage, the organization entertains discussions on monument building—ostentatious facilities, shrines to the past, and so on. Rather than rewarding prophets and entrepreneurs, the group suddenly rewards those who are compliant and benign. Denial of reality undermines the health of the group; those who strive to address reality pay a price for their honesty and courage.

Operational and team builders are usually in charge. The types of leaders that dominate during this phase are usually operational and team-building leaders. Although their gifts are important, without the motivating visionary and the strategic thinker guiding the way, the group degenerates into an arrogant, well-oiled social club. To lead an organization out of this morass will require the emergence of a directing leader who gets insiders excited about a new vision—preferably one that builds on the vision that has been completely or mostly achieved. In most cases a strategic leader is indispensable in developing the plan for resuscitating the group.

Disability

If the stagnation phase runs unchecked, the inevitable result is transition into a state of disability. In this phase the organization is dysfunctional and conflicted. Paranoia, fear, mistrust, and petty infighting prevail. The organization takes on a victim mentality, and survival is grasped for with the organization's final breaths. Those who lead these organizations wind up pursuing political stability rather than new ideas and creative energy. Because funding becomes a problem—who wants to invest in a dying entity?—the organization sells out for any purpose that breeds resources. The core vision is a distant memory; the survival instinct rules.

A unique strategic leader must take over. It is virtually impossible to turn around such an organization. Our research suggests that it takes a very special kind of leader—someone who has the strategic aptitude, is experienced yet relatively young, has tremendous self-confidence, is willing to stick it out over the long haul, and can project vision and values without expending all available energy on that function. If people can be shaken out of their fear and lethargy and into a state of hope, then this leader has the potential to right the ship. In every case we have studied, the individual who led the organization into the stagnation and disability phases has proven incapable of directing the organization to health. In other words, it always takes a new, more effective leader to restore health—if that is even possible.

These types of turnarounds typically consume a minimum of four years' time and exhaust the leader and the leader's family. We have also learned that a turnaround specialist is good for one or two of these in their lifetime; a third attempt, even after two prior successes, usually overcomes the individual. Providing such leadership is incredibly depleting of mental and emotional energy. Never take on a turnaround in this state unless you are called and committed beyond reason; it is not "just a job" or "a chance for some good experience." In such cases it becomes a leader's graveyard.

Unless a strong turnaround leader enters the picture, the organization eventually dies. The recognition of death takes longer in churches and nonprofits because of the tax laws and other structural distinctions compared to business, but death is the inevitable result.

AVOIDING THE DECLINE STAGES

Once an organization hits stagnation, recovery is difficult. The more time it spends in that state, the less likely such a recovery becomes. Naturally, the best way to deal with the dangers of stagnation (and, subsequently, disability) is never to get to that point. Is it an inevitable state for organizations to experience?

Unlike human beings, organizations need not die if they have effective leadership that continually brings renewal to the group. There are three important steps to facilitating continued health over the long haul.

First, the organization must increase its development of additional leaders. In order to maintain its existing level of strength and to continue to expand, leaders will be needed. The failure to produce capable and equipped leaders will prevent the organization from moving forward; deterioration and decline will be the inescapable result.

Second, leaders must have access to reliable information about the state of the organization and the context in which it operates. An important leadership function is to regularly assess how the organization is doing and what blind spots, unforeseen obstacles, or untapped opportunities are emerging. With each passing day the potential for dissipation grows; leaders must diligently protect against decline and pursue health.

Among the most common signs of nascent decline include: being on the verge of seeing the original vision fulfilled (and thereby losing the impetus to continue); the recentralizing of power under the founder (signaling fear of irrelevance or lost purpose, which triggers excessive control by the founder); and an imbalance among the structure, quality of performance, and level of productivity. The presence of any one of these may indicate the onset of decline.

Finally, continued health is fostered by "curve jumping." This is the practice of rebirthing or redirecting the organization as it nears fulfillment of the vision. If you were to graph the development of your organization over time, you would probably see a classic bell-shaped curve. The time represented by the slope of the curve flattening out—that is, at a point in time somewhat prior to when the organization peaks—is the prime moment to initiate a new strategic thrust. The goal is to exploit the existing strengths produced by the recent growth in order to introduce a new vision or idea that renews people's interest and energy in where things are headed.

This renewal process may well return the group to the infancy phase and the pursuit of a new set of outcomes, transitioning people's energy and allegiance to the new ideal. That new initiative might be a spinoff organization (for example, a church plant or extension, a parachurch ministry spawned by the church, or a specialty organization birthed through your existing business), or a new, noncompetitive organization (an acquisition or an unrelated start-up).

One reason that so many organizations reach the top of the curve and enter the decline stages is because curve jumping is difficult. Not only must the leaders be tending to the current needs of the organization, they must also be anticipating what it will take for the group to be healthy and growing several steps down the road. In other words, once you hit the growth phase, it is time for the directing and strategic leaders to allocate some of their time and expertise to conceiving the new curve. That is feasible because the expansion phase shifts more of the leadership responsibilities onto the plates of the team-building and operational leaders; consequently, the "excess capacity" of the directing and strategic leaders can be devoted to the long-term health of the organization.

LESSONS ON LIFE CYCLES

Perhaps you noticed that each of the stages ushered in a new set of challenges and difficulties for leaders to face. The question is not whether an organization has problems; even the healthiest and best-led organizations encounter problems. The key is to discover the nature of the problem, how the organization handles it, the stage in the life cycle at which the problem occurs, and the implications of the emergence of that specific problem given the organization's present place on the development continuum. Examining these factors can help you diagnose if the problem is natural and if it is handled in a healthy manner, or if the problem is a sign of unexpected weakness and is addressed in ways that will produce additional (and unnecessary) challenges.

Knowing Aptitude Is Crucial

You can also see how helpful it is to understand your leadership aptitude (as described in chapter 3) and the ebb and flow nature of the partnership with leaders who possess complementary aptitudes. Accurately assessing both your aptitude and the stage of development in which the organization finds itself opens up a powerful mechanism for knowing what combination of leaders and skills may be best suited to the group's needs at that moment in time. If you are willing to flex in terms of levels of authority and responsibility according to the group's stage in the life cycle, then the chance of facilitating a healthy organization is significantly enhanced.

My research on life cycles and leadership has also shown that the larger an organization becomes, the more likely it is that different sectors of the organization—for example, its various departments, programs, divisions—will reach various points on the curve at different times. This uneven growth pattern requires divergent leadership responses within the group simultaneously.

> *If today's organizations are to serve us well, they require not only people who can play the kind of leadership role [they can handle], but people who are able and willing to stop playing that role at the appropriate time.*
>
> —JOHN KOTTER

Take, for example, a twenty-five-year-old church. The evangelism program may be one of the most mature ministries in the church and approaching the balance stage. It is time for the leaders of the evangelism ministry to conceive and prepare to launch a new evangelism initiative that will renew people's energy for gospel outreach. The community service ministry, however, may just be entering the expansion phase, which demands different leadership. The ministry to youth may be stuck in an advanced state of infancy, a situation that is not unusual but that cries out for serious leadership intervention to prevent the youth program from burning out before reaching a healthy, growing, sustainable part on the curve.

Take a look at the organization in which you are a leader. Examining the entire organization, at what stage is it today? How well is it positioned to enter that next phase? And how about the various programs and departments within the organization? Are they all equipped with leaders who know where their portion of the organization stands and how to move it forward most reasonably? Effective leadership—the right blend of leadership introduced at the proper moment—is critical for healthy growth and lasting impact.

Uncomfortable Questions

- How is life cycle measurement carried out in your organization? Whose responsibility is it, and how seriously do people take the results?
- If you have already gone through a curve jumping phase, what were the key lessons you learned from that experience that will help you to be more effective at it next time?
- As you consider your leadership within the organization, how sensitive are you to the profile you should or should not have within the group as a result of the place on the life cycle continuum?

—Epilogue—

> People are often led to causes and become committed to great ideas through persons who personify those ideas. They have to find the embodiment of the idea in flesh and blood in order to commit themselves to it.
>
> —Martin Luther King Jr.

EPILOGUE

Obedience, Not Success

*A*S JESUS STARTED ON HIS WAY, a man ran up to him and fell on his knees. "Good teacher," he asked, "what must I do to be a great leader who is Christian?"

"Why do you call me good?" Jesus answered. "No one is good except God alone. You know the requirements: cast God's vision, motivate people to pursue it, mobilize them efficiently, strategically guide their efforts, and develop the resources necessary to fulfill the vision."

"Teacher," he declared, "all these I have done since I have been a leader."

Jesus looked at him and loved him. "One thing you lack," he said. "Change your philosophy of leadership from achieving success to being obedient, and you will truly be useful to your Father in heaven."

At this the man's face fell. He went away because he had great success in leadership.

Jesus looked around and said to his disciples, "How hard it is for the leaders of this world to lead in ways that honor God."[1]

A Fish Out of Water

Some people dread hearing words like *you're ugly* or *you're stupid*. What are the reactions you most dread? For me, the ultimate nightmare would be to hear God review my life and conclude, *You achieved great success in the eyes of people, but you were not obedient to my leading of you. How hard it is for the leaders of the world to lead in ways that honor me.*

Most of us who lead people get caught up in the world's definitions of success and greatness. Leadership often seems overwhelming as we study the challenges, observe the inappropriate choices of people (even Christian people), determine what it will take to bring about desired change, and wonder how we are possibly going to facilitate the outcomes that we have set as our goals.

Jesus was a leader on a mission, too, and his mandate obviously far exceeded anything you or I might hope to facilitate. In the course of following through on his plan, he provided a wealth of lessons for leaders—lessons that conflict with much of the world's leadership wisdom:

A leader is a servant. Those whose goal it is to be first will be last. No student is above his teacher or servant greater than his master. The greatest act is that of love. Blessed are the meek, for they will inherit the earth. Your words matter. Love your enemies and pray for those who persecute you. Do not worry about tomorrow. Do not judge others. Count the cost. You will be persecuted if you represent Christ well. You must have faith to accomplish things of value. Reconcile your differences rather than gain revenge or hold a grudge. Treat everyone fairly. People will always challenge your authority. Stand up for those who cannot take care of themselves. Stand firm for what you believe and what you have been sent to do.

Sometimes, when I read those principles and compare them to my own brand of leadership, I get depressed. The gap between the Lord's lessons and my best performance is so large. Do you ever feel that way?

During the two months preceding the writing of this book I traveled the country to speak with a number of key Christian leaders regarding the future of the church and what we, as leaders, might do to most effectively bring about transformation. Two of the leaders whom I most respect gave me fabulous insight and encouragement. But the most important lesson I gleaned came from statements they both made at the end of our conversations.

They had not conferred with each other; in fact, neither even knew that I was meeting with the other, so I know there was no conspiracy! They spoke on different days, in different cities, in different contexts. Yet their message was almost identical.

"At the end of the day," the first great leader told me, "I review what I've done and try to figure out if I've been obedient to what God called me to do. If I was, then I sleep well."

"Mother Teresa gave me this plaque," said the other leader, moving some papers on his desk to reveal a long, narrow desk plate. "I keep it on my desk, facing me, at all times." The plaque simply reads "Obedience, Not Success."

In the final analysis, I think perhaps my biggest issue is that too often my philosophy of effective leadership loses touch with God's reality. I want so badly to be used by God to fulfill the vision he has given to me to facilitate transformation. When there are no overt or measurable indications of such outcomes, I get frustrated. But that frustration ought not intimidate, paralyze, anger, or redirect me. Ultimately, it's God's war to win, not mine. I am simply a soldier with orders to carry out. My job is to faithfully show up every day, ready for action, obedient to the direction he provides.

Leading for the applause of the world is about gaining popularity, making money, taking over market share, leaving a legacy. Leading for God is about obedience to his vision and principles. That is not an excuse for a lack of excellence or setting your sights low. We represent him in whatever venue we find ourselves with the privilege of leading people. But the results are really his to determine. He is in control; we're not. It is his Holy Spirit that transforms people and situations, not us.

My prayer is that as you strive to lead people—whether on Wall Street or

Main Street, in the boardroom or your living room, in God's house or the White House—you will always focus on his calling to you and be true to the vision he has revealed to you. Remember that he is more glorified by your character than by anything you may be able to achieve. You may work on developing your competencies so that he can accomplish great things through your service. In the end, leadership is about serving God by blessing people through the fulfillment of the vision he entrusts to you. Stay focused on him and he will use you in great ways, whether your opportunities come in the workplace, the church, or other places. Your leadership matters to God because you matter to God.

Let your leadership be an act of worship to God, a service to people, and a source of joy within you. What a wonderful honor we have in leading for the glory of God!

BIBLIOGRAPHY

Adizes, Ichak. *Corporate Life cycles.* Englewood Cliffs, N.J.: Prentice-Hall, 1988.

Barna, George. *The Power of Team Leadership.* Colorado Springs: WaterBrook Press, 2001.

_____. *The Second Coming of the Church.* Nashville, Tenn.: Word Books, 1998.

_____, editor and contributor. *Leaders on Leadership.* Ventura, Calif.: Regal Books, 1998.

_____. *Turning Vision into Action.* Ventura, Calif.: Regal Books, 1996.

_____. *The Power of Vision.* Ventura, Calif.: Regal Books, 1992.

Bennis, Warren and Burt Nanus. *Leaders: The Strategies for Taking Charge.* New York: Harper & Row Publishers, 1985.

Bennis, Warren. *On Becoming a Leader.* Reading, Mass.: Addison-Wesley Publishing, 1989.

Blanchard, Ken, Bill Hybels, and Phil Hodges. *Leadership by the Book.* Colorado Springs: WaterBrook Press, 1999.

Conger, Jay. *Learning to Lead.* San Francisco: Jossey-Bass Publishers, 1992.

Coser, Lewis. *The Functions of Social Conflict.* New York: Free Press, 1956.

Ford, Leighton. *Transforming Leadership.* Downers Grove, Ill.: InterVarsity Press, 1991.

Garten, Jeffrey. *The Mind of the C.E.O.* New York: Basic Books, 2001.

Guinness, Os. *Character Counts.* Grand Rapids, Mich.: Baker Books, 1999.

Handy, Charles. *The Empty Raincoat.* London: Arrow Business Books, 1995.

_____. *The Age of Unreason.* Boston: Harvard Business School Press, 1989.

Hesselbein, Frances and Paul Cohen, eds. *Leader to Leader.* San Francisco: Jossey-Bass, 1999.

Hoffer, Eric. *The True Believer: Thoughts on the Nature of Mass Movements.* New York: Harper & Row, 1951.

Hunter, James Davison. *The Death of Character.* New York: Basic Books, 2000.

Josephson, Michael and Wes Hanson, eds. *The Power of Character.* San Francisco: Jossey-Bass, 1998.

Karrass, Chester. *The Negotiating Game.* New York: Harper Business, 1992.

Katzenbach, Jon and Douglas Smith. *The Wisdom of Teams.* New York: Harper Business, 1993.

Kouzes, James and Barry Posner. *The Leadership Challenge.* San Francisco: Jossey-Bass, 1995.

Krzyzewski, Mike. *Leading with the Heart.* New York: Warner Books, 2000.

Mannoia, Kevin. *The Integrity Factor.* Indianapolis, Ind.: Life and Life Communications, 1996.

Miller, Lawrence. *Barbarians to Bureaucrats.* New York: Potter Publishing, 1989.

Nanus, Burt. *Visionary Leadership.* San Francisco: Jossey-Bass, 1992.

Nixon, Richard. *Leaders.* New York: Simon & Schuster, 1990.

Bibliography

Novak, Michael. *Business as a Calling.* New York: Free Press, 1996.

Ogilvy, David. *An Autobiography.* New York: John Wiley & Sons, 1997.

Pascale, Richard. *Managing on the Edge.* New York: Simon & Schuster, 1990.

Sande, Ken. *The Peacemaker.* Grand Rapids, Mich.: Baker Books, 1997.

Sanders, J. Oswald. *Spiritual Leadership.* Chicago: Moody Press, 1980.

Senge, Peter. *The Fifth Discipline.* New York: Doubleday Currency, 1990.

Sheehy, Gail. *Character: America's Search for Leadership.* New York: William Morrow and Company, 1988.

Spears, Larry, ed. *Insights on Leadership.* New York: John Wiley & Sons, 1998.

Wills, Garry. *Certain Trumpets.* New York: Simon & Schuster, 1994.

Wilson, James Q. *On Character.* Washington, D.C.: AEI Press, 1995.

APPENDIX

ABOUT THE BARNA RESEARCH GROUP, LTD.

*T*HE BARNA RESEARCH GROUP is located in Ventura, California, and is a full-service marketing research company dedicated to serving the information needs of clients by providing "current, accurate and reliable information, in bite-sized pieces, at reasonable cost, to facilitate strategic decision-making."

Established in 1984 by George and Nancy Barna, the company has been honored to serve thousands of clients through primary research, consulting, and seminar, working with for-profit and nonprofit organizations. Among the for-profit clients served are American Express, Federal Express, Ford Motor Company, Hyatt Hotels, Pearle Vision Centers, Ramada Inns, Southwestern Bell Telephone, Visa U.S.A., and The Walt Disney Company. Among the nonreligious, nonprofit organizations served have been Boys & Girls Clubs, CARE, Easter Seals, Feed the Children, KidsPeace, and the U.S. Army. Barna Research has served several thousand churches and more than three hundred parachurch ministries such as American Bible Society, Billy Graham Association, Campus

A Fish Out of Water

Crusade for Christ, Compassion International, Focus on the Family, InterVarsity, Josh McDowell Ministries, Prison Fellowship, Salvation Army, World Vision, and Youth for Christ.

The organization is well known for helping Christian ministries stay alert to changes and opportunities in American society. The group develops resources for Christian ministries and provides a wealth of free, current information on-line, including the publication of its latest findings in a free biweekly report (*The Barna Update*). More than one million copies of resources produced by Barna Research have been purchased to help organizations be more effective in their work.

To learn more about Barna Research, please visit www.barna.org or call 1-800-55-BARNA.

DISTANCE LEARNING THROUGH BARNA UNIVERSITY

Would you like to receive the best leadership training available? Would you like your teachers to be some of the nation's finest practitioners in ministry leadership? Would you like that training to be delivered to your place of work, at a reasonable cost?

If so, Barna University was created with you in mind!

Here's how it works. Barna University will provide eight learning sessions each year through satellite and Internet technology. Each session is taught by an experienced, highly regarded practitioner whose track record underscores his or her expertise. The emphasis of each session will be developing the skills and insights that every leader needs to be effective. In addition to the unique, interactive, satellite-delivered teaching sessions, you will have the following benefits:

- on-line readings, references, and application exercises developed exclusively for Barna University students to help in absorbing the key principles and skills addressed during the teaching session;
- no charge for additional individuals from your organization participating in the training process at the same location;

Appendix

- a bulletin board for interaction with other students;
- CEUs available from accredited institutions; and
- discounts on related products.

Sessions are being added constantly. Among the topics addressed in sessions are effective team-building, current cultural trends, leadership development strategies, leading in a postmodern era, leadership as servanthood, handling family pressures, improving your strategic thinking, conflict as a leadership tool, personal character, leadership transitions, measuring success, leadership endurance, and much more.

Barna University's "revolving faculty" include many of the nation's most dynamic Christian leaders. Each session is hosted by George Barna, the Directing Leader of the Barna Research Group, and incorporates real-time interaction with students from across the nation. For a listing of forthcoming sessions, visit www.barna.org.

The annual enrollment fee is just a fraction of what you would pay in registration, travel, and expenses if you were to attend similar seminars featuring these leaders. Barna University represents more than great education; it's good stewardship, too.

If you would like more information about how to grow into the leadership shoes that God provided for you, contact Barna Research at 1-800-55-BARNA. The nation's premier leaders want to share their wisdom with you.

BARNA UNIVERSITY

Helping You Become the Leader God Intended You to Be

NOTES

INTRODUCTION

1. Matthew 5:13.

CHAPTER ONE

1. Warren Bennis and Burt Nanus, *Leaders* (New York: Harper & Row Publishers, 1985), 21.

2. I am not suggesting that non-leader pastors leave the ministry or even that they leave their church. Instead, they may recognize who they are in Christ and how he has gifted and called them, and use their non-leadership gifts to assist the true leaders in developing a healthy, wholistic ministry. Every great leader needs effective communicators and teachers to build up the body of Christ. Teamwork was one of the hallmarks of Jesus' ministry, and thus it should be one of the hallmarks of how we conduct ministry, too.

CHAPTER TWO

1. There are many gifts tests and related commentaries on spiritual gifts. You may wish to review such books as Bruce Bugbee, *What You Do Best in the Body of Christ* (Grand Rapids, Mich.: Zondervan, 1995) or C. Peter Wagner, *Your Spiritual Gifts* (Ventura, Calif.: Regal Books, 1994).

   To specifically ascertain if you have the gift of leadership, you may wish to take the Christian Leader Profile, available through the Barna Research

Group. The Profile is an inventory that helps you to evaluate your call to leadership, the quality of your character and leadership competencies, and your leadership aptitude. You may purchase and complete it on-line, at www.barna.org.

2. The initial section of the Christian Leader Profile poses a series of questions related to these very issues to help you discern whether God has called you to be a habitual leader.

CHAPTER THREE

1. More information about the Christian Leader Profile can be obtained from the Barna Research Group Web site, at www.barna.org.

CHAPTER FOUR

1. See my book *The Power of Vision* (Ventura, Calif.: Regal Books, 1992).
2. Corporate Vision Statements That Leaders in the Bible Could Have Developed:

Abraham (Genesis 12:1–3; 13:15; 15:18): To lead the Israelites to inhabit a new land chosen by God, to worship God alone, and to bless others at all times.

Moses (Exodus 3:7–10; Deuteronomy 26:16–19): To lead the Israelites to live in a place free from religious oppression and to follow a new moral code that honors God and shows love of other people.

Joshua (Joshua 1:1–9): To implement innovative military strategy, guided by God, toward conquering and settling the promised land and developing a society that adheres to God's Law.

Josiah (2 Kings 23:21–25): To eradicate all traces of idolatry, restore scriptural justice and righteousness, and re-establish the preeminence of God and his ways.

Notes

Nehemiah (Nehemiah 2:17; 9:13): To restore the nation of Israel by rebuilding the walls of Jerusalem and introducing religious reforms and spiritual revival among the Israelites.

Paul (Romans 15:16–20; Galatians 2:7–10; Ephesians 3:7–12): To lead Gentiles to faith in Christ, planting new churches throughout the Roman Empire that emphasize spiritual purity and reproduction.

Peter (Acts 2:11–12, 14; 4:32–35): To evangelize Jews in Jerusalem and develop a new community of Jewish disciples of Christ.

3. A more extensive discussion of the vision development and implementation process is contained in my book *Turning Vision into Action* (Ventura, Calif.: Regal Books, 1996).

CHAPTER FIVE

1. Warren Bennis, "The Character of Leadership," in Michael Josephson and Wes Hanson, eds., *The Power of Character* (San Francisco: Jossey-Bass, 1998), 143–44.
2. From Matthew 15:17-20.
3. Gail Sheehy, *Character: America's Search for Leadership* (New York: William Morrow, 1988), 20–21.
4. In particular, see 1 Timothy 3 and Titus 1 for Paul's teachings on leadership character.
5. Josephson and Hanson, *The Power of Character*, 4.
6. 1 Timothy 3:5.
7. You might consider using the Christian Leader Profile, the self-assessment tool we've already mentioned, which contains a section that explores your character and identifies dimensions that require greater attention. For more information go to the Barna Research Group Web site, at www.barna.org.

CHAPTER SIX

1. Be clear that I am not suggesting people's self-worth be based solely upon what they produce or accomplish. Our self-worth is based upon God's redemption and acceptance. We have value because he values us, not because of what we do. Using our spiritual standing in Christ as the basis of our self-worth and adopting his vision for our life then enables us to gain further joy through what we are able to do in serving him.

CHAPTER EIGHT

1. I Samuel 13:14; Acts 13:22.
2. Genesis 32:22–32.
3. See Matthew 25:34–36, 40. Other descriptions of the compassionate focus we may take include, but are not limited to, Matthew 19:21; Acts 6:1–4; I Timothy 5:3; and James 1:27.

EPILOGUE

1. This "faux parable" is based on the real words of Jesus found in Mark 10:17–23.